# THE
# MIRROR PARADOX

# FRANKLYN MORRISON

*THE MIRROR PARADOX*

ISBN 978-1-7770465-0-7

Cover design by Sara Derksen

Cover art ©Sara Derksen

# THE MIRROR PARADOX

By Franklyn Morrison

# Dedications

This book is dedicated to all the readers who are searching for their truth.

# The Mirror Paradox

## Table of Contents

# Preface

It pains me sometimes to see how things didn't work out. But if they weren't supposed to work out and they didn't, I need to change my perception. Is that really something "not working out" or is it working out beautifully?

Every success and every failure offer a concrete example of your chosen expectations in that particular situation. Perhaps you can just expect to try, then you can succeed every time you go out there! A good friend of mine, Reiki Grand Master Quinn Straza, tells a great joke. How do you make God laugh? Tell him your plans. Your plans are silent expectations of success or failure. In other words, it's important to shift from having plans to goals and desires. Understand that nothing happens in a day. Things take time. Always trust that the Universe will have your back.

In retrospect, I was constantly trying to be the man other people needed me to be, which was dangerous and counterproductive for my self-growth. I am now working on becoming the man that *I* need to be: no more codependency, no more guilt, or obligations. I need *me* in my life. If you don't show up tomorrow, I still need to be there. If you can't breathe for me or beat my heart, I need to do that. I'm taking responsibility for everything -- especially not having this realization sooner. Embrace the divine. Be the divine masculine or divine feminine you need to be. Buddha renounced all teachers and ultimately, he was his own best teacher. We can all learn something from that. I cherish everyone in my path. They have individually led me through exponential growth.

So, please do yourself a favor and face all your fears! The fears of being alone. You can find yourself when you embrace being alone. The fears of rejection. Anyone rejecting you is doing you a favor by exiting your life. The fear of failure. Most successful people have failed more times than you've tried. The fear of success. Know you're worthy of what you seek. Nothing can take away the drive inside of you. The fear of acceptance. You have to be the first person to accept yourself. Then hold yourself to that standard. The fear of the unknown. The fear of change. When you're in an uncomfortable situation, it's time to face this fear the most and face it head on. Are things not going great in your current lifestyle? It's time to face that fear. This fear of change exacerbates on the other fears and it can hold you down.

When you're searching for yourself you need to ask yourself, what's my main motivation? If you're seeing a lot of fear coming up that's blocking you from seeing your main motivation, maybe your motivation currently needs to face that fear? What are your obstacles in life? What are your goals in life? Are you ready to face the unknown? The unknown is scary and ugly sometimes. Yet it can also be the most beautiful.

How do you transmute fear into power? You allow the fear to know you see it. You let the fear know you're scared. Love yourself just for being able to see that fear. Forgive yourself for not facing the fear sooner. When you do this, you'll fully face your emotions, so you won't hide from them. I want to lead you into the fire, the fire that will burn off any of the old stagnant unneeded parts of yourself that are left. Don't attach yourself to any outcome-- just expect change. When you're unattached to any outcome, just start flowing through life with your truth. When you hold the image of success in a particular area, you attach an expectation to that success. Just be unattached and live without those expectations. As a result, something magical will happen. The unexpected is the most magical occurrence that can happen.

Accept that your thoughts co-create the life you live. Change those thoughts, and you can transform for a more positive outcome.

# Introduction

## What's the Mirror Paradox?

It isn't liking a Justin Timberlake song! The Mirror Paradox is the reflection of our own actions, reactions, views, belief systems, and ways of life. How we react directly shows us what and where we need to heal. What we attract is what we are, since we don't attract opposites. In fact, "like attracts like." We are electrical beings, so our signals are received by other beings on the same frequency. We aren't magnets, electronics, or gadgets. Our intuition guides us through every obstacle to heal our soul. Should we choose to heal our soul, that's the destiny within all of us. Every obstacle we encounter in life is demonstrating patterns to us. If we ignore those patterns, we're ignoring our own healing. Should we choose to see the patterns, we can then guide ourselves to live a happier, healthier, and more fruitful life. We can harness the things that have happened for us as a catalyst for our growth. When we see the positive in the things that happen for us, we then turn ourselves back to the gratitude state.

Finding that state of gratitude has taken me out of suffering. I've struggled for the good of all lessons in this book. I've learned to honor myself, to release everything and to continue to release everything. I've mastered the life changing importance of gratitude. I'll explain the "Two Monster's" society created to hold you back. I've also learned the importance to release the labels of good and bad. In this book I talk about radical acceptance of the things that happen for you. I also discuss what we really need to survive. Finally, I explain the Mirror Paradox and how it applies to everyday situations and how you can heal yourself fully using the Mirror Paradox.

This isn't a book for people who are on the path of denial. This is a book for readers to help recognize that your life is in your control. What you become will always be a combination of what you think and what you do. The Law of Attraction applies here. You can dream until your third eye is fully awoken, but with no action dreams are just dreams. Imagine dreaming up a beautiful movie script with intelligently drawn out character arcs and a storyline that twists at every frame change. But now you have just a dream. What you do with that dream will be determine how you define your life. How will you define your life and take back the control of your healing?

# Chapter 1

## Honor Thy Self

You don't know what other people have endured, so if you are living in a comparative mindset, stop! You can't simplify your version of yourself to them, and they can't simplify their version to you. What have they been through? How is their internal programming different? Nothing can be compared to anyone. Comparison is as simple as saying good and bad. Nothing happens to you; it happens for you. Maybe the fact that your life has been "harder" is all for a reason? But harder compared to whom? Someone will always have it worse. If your belief system isn't working anymore, get rid of it! You don't need to choose anyone else's path. Walk the truth you're supposed to walk. Get rid of the "woe is me" mentality. There's always a light at the end of the tunnel. Don't close the door to the hallway that leads to that light. Remain positive in every situation and the Mirror Paradox will give you more positive situations. "It is what it is" offers a great mindset if you're trying to detach from suffering. But a bad mentality if it's causing you to stop trying. If you want to attract better, be better. If you want more, do more. If you're ready for an easier road, remove the road blocks.

Honoring yourself will be doing the best you can do. There will be circumstances where your best is different in every single waking moment, day, month, and year. But your effort solely determines your success not just your thoughts. How many people want to sit on the sidelines and watch everyone else have fun? Not a lot. Unless you're writing about it!

For example, I used to work a job 40 hours a week doing hard physical labor. I wasn't honoring my abilities to help people in a more productive way. I didn't have the physique to work a job like that. I ended up tired, sore, and unhappy. Sure, I was paying the bills, but I was in passive suicide mode by not honoring the intelligent being that was deep down inside. Honoring yourself goes to a part that society has made you suppress. Honoring yourself means something uniquely different to each individual: some may be able to work 40 hours a week. Some may need to cut their work week to 30 hours a week to fully be able to take care of themselves.

Whose thoughts control your life? Are you being run by the programming everyone else has given you? Has society led you down a dark hallway out of screaming distance? Can someone else really know what's best for you? These are the innate questions you need to sit and ask yourself. Each question holds validity to your truth and your version of yourself. Let's start with whose thoughts control your life; when you realize we're programmed as visual learners from the time we start school, you begin to get an idea of where you lost your truth. Everything is written on a white board or a slide and they point to it with a stick as if to say "learn this' it's very important". But is it really important for who you need to become? Let's talk about what's important in what they taught you. Maybe some math will help you better balance your budget or having good oral skills will help you navigate personal and professional relationships? History isn't your truth. They use certain subjects to blindside you into thinking you're on the good guys' team! This is where the manipulation begins.

Education and modern-day parenting are so dualistic. This is good; therefore, it's right. This is bad; thus, it's wrong. But that's someone else imposing his or her truth into your consciousness. You're at a pivotal moment right now where you get to decide what your values really are. Take those values and run with them. Your values are the intrinsic way to the roadmap of how you really feel inside. I use the word "intrinsic" because it's very much interlinked into your emotions. Famous psychologist Abraham Maslow talks about getting to the root of Intrinsic Motivation. Intrinsic Motivation is taking the necessary leap into action when taking ownership of your dreams.

Your emotions - good or bad - can give you an outburst of anger, sadness, or laughing until you cry with so much joy. So how do you reclaim your thoughts as your own? How do you create your own truth when you've been given such false ideals from everyone you've ever learned from in life? This is something that plagued me. You have to fully release everyone's opinion of you and everything they hold value to, ever. What does this mean? Another person's opinion is very useful, but it isn't your truth. One's opinion is useful to what degree you want to have someone in your life once you've fully discovered your truth.

I constantly tell myself a don Miguel Ruiz quote from his book, *The Voice of Knowledge*. *"Don't listen to the lies others tell you, don't listen to the lies you tell yourself."* These are the lies; these lies bind you from discovering who you're really supposed to be. So why is there so much hype in school, getting the perfect job, having the perfect relationship, etc.? These are things that society has created to keep you searching, keep you blinded. *"Don't listen to the lies!"*

In my own journey, I had a house, a wife, a 100k a year job, a new truck, but I was miserable. What society should teach you is to seek happiness within yourself. Once I started to realize none of that stuff mattered to me, then the real crisis started. Then there was the internal crisis of how to turn my life around and continue to be successful. Mind you, at the time I didn't know success was an internal job either. I was still being blinded by society's teachings of having to have material wealth. Even though I had rejected the material wealth that I'd earned in life, I was still blind to what success actually meant.

Additionally, school taught me that I wasn't good at math. School showed me I was bad at English and had a poor attention span. What school didn't show me is that I needed to engage myself in a different way. Maybe school worked better for other people, but as a highly creative person who needs to turn everything into an art project, it failed me. It's not like I was failing, but I wasn't doing great either. I barely passed my high school math classes. I left high school thinking I was bad at math and couldn't do a job that required math. Once I entered a technical school to learn how to become an electronics technician, I realized that being bad at math was the farthest thing from the truth. Now that I had a reason to engage in math more fully and actual reasons to solve the equations, I found out I was great at math. So maybe school should have taught me to question peoples' evaluation of me and I could have come to my own conclusion that I wasn't being taught in a way that I could understand?

What's my point of all of this? I listened to what they told me and took it to heart as being the truth. I believed that it was the truth when the fact was: they shouldn't have been giving me a prognosis. Have you ever been to the doctor when you were told something is wrong and you need to take some medications? I have and sometimes I believed it. I often flat out said, "Doc, you're full of it." Within some of those occasions, I didn't take the medications and miraculously got better. You know yourself very intuitively. You need to trust that. Your truth will tell if you're really sick or if your sickness is a symptom of something else. All of your truth can be found in a state of aloneness. In the state of aloneness, you'll be able to comfortably disregard everyone's opinions and see clearly between the lines.

Aloneness is a state of being comfortable in your solitude. It's the contrast to loneliness. People will often ask, "Don't you get bored by yourself? What do you do?" The truth is, once you start to find the inner peace, you no longer seek out the demons that stir your soul. This inner peace is calmness indescribable to those who haven't been seeking it out. When you find a calm comfortable state of aloneness, you're whole, you don't seek the answers from outside but within.

The answers are always in your heart. Most of the chatter in your brain is from other people. Other ideals enter your conscious and subconscious minds. Basically, everything you've learned up to this point makes up what you're currently agreeing to, whether it involves politics, religions, faith, and/or whatever codes of conduct you live by currently. By erasing everything you're learned and seeking the inner wisdom in your heart, you can find a comfortable state of aloneness.

Aloneness can transcend growth to a level you wouldn't have known your capable of achieving. Once you find this state, you might realize all of your ideology can change. Tapping into your heart space is tapping into your soul. All of the knowledge from previous lifetimes is attainable in one breath. All of your previous beliefs can disappear in an instant. When you start recalling your soul information, you can no longer be racist. You can no longer be sexist. You can live with compassion for everyone and everything. How can you no longer be racist or sexist? When you enter the comfortable state of aloneness, you've connected with your heart. In this space when you listen to your heart, you only hear love back. Your heart doesn't have the ability to hate. When you enter the heart space, you start feeling one consciousness. One consciousness is the connection to everyone and everything. It's an amazing place to be in. You can start to think past yourself and think about others on such a deep level. This is the beauty of finding your truth, the beauty of aloneness.

Have you ever heard the saying, "Only love is real?" What's that actually referring to? Being in your heart space. Your heart can't feel hate, or dismay. Your heart is the path to your truth. When

16

you follow your heart, you'll start attracting others that follow their hearts as well. Love will be real because you'll be attracting real love, not something learned, not something taught. You'll know what the feeling is for yourself from your own heart. If you're ever at an impasse in life, pause, take a moment, quiet your mind, and ask your heart to tell you what you really feel about a situation. Only that feeling is real. Every other thing going on in your mind is fake. Your heart is your truth, and it'll guide you to finding your answers.

Besides, it's so essential to dissolve right and wrong. Once you see the soul pattern you're playing out, you can realize no one is wrong. In their mind they are doing the best as to their beliefs. The best as to how they were raised and what were taught. At this point we can move the goal posts so to speak. Maybe we put them at an unattainable distance? Or perhaps we made them way too close? By remembering what you learned in previous lives, you can open up to an enormous amount of information. You can open up to an enormous amount of compassion. You'll open up to an amazing amount of growth. You'll open up to the soul's true potential on this planet.

We're in a constant state of flux, always moving. We grow and change every day. As per what direction, it's completely up to you. You need to do yourself a favor and release everything. By releasing everything you have ever learned you get to clear the slate of your belief system. By embracing aloneness, you get to honor yourself fully. Only in that comfortable state of aloneness can you clear the slate and start fresh. Remember every day you can clear the slate. Every day you get to start again. This is the wonderful miracle you get. When you witness this miracle, embrace it and be grateful for it.

# Chapter 2

## Release Everything

Release everything you've learned and you can come to one very humble conclusion: What do I know? Do I really know anything? You could be 25 or 70 years old and attain this conclusion. Some people never really get to this point in their lives. By telling yourself you don't actually know anything, you can open yourself up to what you need to know to live your truth. So, what do I know? I know an accumulation of the knowledge I've acquired throughout my life. Is it useful if I'm working at 7/11? Not to me. Don't get me wrong, the world needs people to work these jobs. But there's a transition period in life when you can no longer search out a job that's less meaningful to you, as you start to search for your truth.

By getting to the heart of the matter, the fact is the truth is in your heart. Your truth isn't something you've learned from others but from yourself. Your truth can't be expressed in words. Your truth is your feelings of contentment. When you dive deep into knowing yourself fully, you can realize what you feel is real. Have you ever gone on that date that you didn't want to pursue? Or went out with friends when you really wanted to stay home? How did it feel? I bet it felt really uncomfortable. This is your heart speaking to your body telling you your truth.

I once went out against my truth, at a very in tuned state in my body. My body spoke so loudly that I got physically ill and had to leave the date early. This isn't even an extreme example of someone not listening to themselves. We must listen to our body. It tells us so much if we're willing to get to know it. When you do things out of obligation, you start to inject a poison into the event that will only really hurt you. Other people won't know who you truly are because they'll think, "Sally loves doing that, so I don't know why she suddenly didn't want to come tonight." Don't let people have those expectations about you. Remove the guilt from yourself with the learned behaviors. If it isn't suiting you, then you can drop it and change.

You're allowed to change. At any given time, you're allowed to change your mind. Anyone exercising compassion will allow you to shift and change into a different person. Often relationships are based on the circumstances that people share. When your circumstance changes and you need to alter your lifestyle, the friendship will often fail. If this has happened, it wasn't a friendship based on unconditional love but one based on expectation. I remember having a friend, but we stopped going out drinking together and hanging out. I then had the sobering conclusion that we didn't actually have anything in common. We both agreed that the only thing that was the common factor between us was that we both abused the same substance together. That isn't friendship- that's codependency. There's a huge difference. When the word "dependency" is attached the word, it now becomes a word describing addiction, including dysfunctional behaviors.

You're allowed to be different. When you become brutally honest with yourself, you might come to the conclusion that you've never actually been yourself. You've been wearing a mask for twenty or thirty years. It's time to take the mask off and be yourself! That's the greatest gift you can give to yourself. When you give that gift to yourself, you can then start to present the gift of your true self to others. It's only a gift if you're being your true self; otherwise, you're injecting lies into the relationship: a lie that starts with you.

For instance, I'll give you a hint: your true self won't want to hurt anyone. Your true self in your heart center only wants to inject compassion into the lives of others. Your true self doesn't want to cause any pain. Do you like it when others inflict pain on you? If we look at John 8:32 from the Bible, it says, *"The truth shall set you free."* Do yourself a favor and do not attach karmically to others by injecting hurt or poison into their lives. People go through enough just living with the negative self-talk in their own heads. It's as simple as the golden rule. Most people are innocent even when injecting lies into their relationships. They think, I'm Sally, the woman who loves watching TV and drinking a glass of wine after a hard day at the office. Consider if Sally was never given that programming and rejected all of the things she learned. Who would she really be? Would she really have to wind down after work? Would she even work full time? If she was working within her honest limits, she'd be content with a cup of tea. I think the majority of people overwork and over stimulate themselves.

You're allowed to be unique. Why can't you be unique? There are over 7 billion people on this Earth, all unique in their own way. Everyone has something very special to share and teach the world. These teachings are deeply buried in your truth. Sometimes we need to shed every layer of our being and completely empty the glass of who we think we are in order create the "who we need to be person." So, go ahead dump out all the lies you've been taught. Pile them onto the table and pick up the pieces. Rearrange them in a new creation. Sometimes when things fall apart, it's really so they can come back together again. Look where the pieces fall and act accordingly. You can dump it all out and only pick up the pieces you want and make a completely new puzzle. You get to be the architect of your desires and free will.

So, if you lose friendships finding yourself, if you lose a spouse finding yourself, if you lose a career finding yourself, I'm telling you, it's worth it. Because if you lose any of those things trying to find yourself, then it wasn't meant to be. There was a piece of the puzzle jammed into the wrong puzzle. Not even the wrong spot, the wrong puzzle!

Without properly knowing the self, how can one properly honor thy self? What are you then honoring? The unknown. So, remove the negative mindset that's been imprinted on you from others. Remove the lies that others have told you. Please forgive yourself for ever listening to the things you were told. Forgive yourself for honoring the lies others told you. You did the best you could do given the circumstances and scenarios. Now it's time to take back the reins and control your life the way you want to. You get to take full control on your belief system. You can take lessons from it or completely dismiss everything in it. Only in your heart when you void your mind of all words, will you know your own truth. Even what you've learned from this book might have to be dismissed as false when you reach the proper levels of self-realization. I encourage you to do whatever it is you need to do. Only when you start from a place of emptiness can you fill in with what you designate as your truth.

Be careful of your thoughts as they can manifest into the life you live. Be careful, make sure that your thoughts and actions align properly with your truth. What you put up with will tell the Universe how you want to be treated. You only every attract situations and people that hurt you or heal you. If you keep staying in an abusive situation, you'll continue to attract abusive situations. When you stay in a situation like that, you're telling the Universe, "I am willing to put up with this." When you readily walk away from things that no longer hurt you, you can then attract the things that will help you heal. You'll attract things and situations that won't require your healing. That's what this book is about: healing.

How can you heal yourself without needing a doctor?

Your body speaks to you every day and lets you know what you need to stretch and what you need to work on specifically. We have to learn to listen to our body, listen to what it's telling us. Where do we feel the stress? What kind of stress is it? Are we in physical pain? There are so many warning signs we get before having major problems occur. If we embrace that our body is in communication with us, we can use these warning signs to our advantage. Only when we're honest and fully commit can we heal fully.

# Chapter 3

## Tuning In

How do we properly tune into our bodies? We look, listen, feel, and ask. When we look at our distress, we're seeing where it is on our body. Is it embodied in the tension on the front or the back of our body? What body part is hurting? Is it a specific muscle or joint? How do we listen to our body? We pay attention to what we're doing in the present moment. Instead of letting the ego say, "I got this," ease into your movements going deeper into them with your breath. Breathe into the movement. When we're listening, we are feeling. That moment the tension arises we feel it. Stopping before the tension turns into major pain is listening.

How do we ask our body? We check in. I call it a self-check. What am I feeling right now?

Why? Is there a reason I am feeling this way? When you learn to meditate and do it on a regular basis, a self-check can take very little time. We don't need to stop and take a five-minute self-check. It can literally be a few seconds. Ok, everything seems good, but wait, there's some tension in my shoulder. Oh, I was working out yesterday and it's in the target group I was addressing. Carry on as scheduled.  Sometimes it might be a pain in your heart, sometimes a headache. Whatever it is, wherever it is, meditation opens up the road to highway speed self-checks. Yoga tunes your physical and mental bodies together through synchronizing your breath and movement. Meditation is like using the highway to self-check, whereas Yoga is like flying the jet to self-check. If you do neither, you're walking.

I'm a deep believer that everyone encompasses an energy in your body that builds up if not properly released. I'll give you an example. I'm a journey-person electrician, and I was working a job that no longer aligned with my truth. I knew it. I'd go to work every day and be miserable. I'm a great actor, so I could hide my discontent to my employer very well. I pretended that everything was going great. As I started to properly align with myself, I found myself having emotional outbursts. Now this was normal to me at the time. Up to points after leaving that job, I thought my emotions controlling me was merely a normal part of adult life. Well, it isn't. I held onto the idea so strongly of me working at this job and just toughing it out for the rest of my life that it manifested into an injury in my wrist. Your wrist signifies the ease of movement through life. It was my left wrist. Your left side is your personal side, your feminine side. So, I was stopping the ease of movement through life.

One month before that major sprain happened, I got a piece of metal in my eye. Like what was I not seeing? It was in my left eye. What was I not seeing for myself? The Universe was willing to literally throw things right into my face for me to see that I wasn't looking ahead clearly in life, thus manifesting a very painful eye injury. After it healed, I continued on to work like everything was great. All of these accidents were freak accidents and don't even logically make sense. I wore the proper personal protective equipment I was slowly exiting out of passive suicide mode by taking better care of my body through eating right and exercise. But none the less, I was lying to myself about how I wanted to hold onto the past and not look clearly into the future. I was lying to myself about how I wanted to create my future.

Life is all or nothing. You can't have each foot on two boats going opposite directions. Life will show you how to properly align yourself through hardships and pain. The trick is to take that pain and suffering and use it as a catalyst for a higher purpose. Your purpose! Your growth is dependent on your actions. You need to work at the transition to a higher purpose career once you have this moment of realization. There are very intimate moments you'll have in your life with yourself. How will you deal with these moments and use them to your advantage? Remember the hardships that you endure. They're there for a reason. Those hardships are for your growth. You're not a victim to anyone. You're a product of the work you do manifesting from thoughts and actions.

When you do a self-check and you're feeling good, then get to work. If you're completely miserable, note that down. This is your body telling you, you're out of alignment on a professional level. This misalignment is going to start causing you physical stress. Take it from me all the money in the world isn't worth that stress you put on yourself. So, you make enough money that you can afford a psychologist, but if you didn't work that job you wouldn't need one. Knowing your worth and honoring your time directly align. You have to show the Universe you're willing to put yourself first. When you put out the signal that you don't care about your physical or mental health, you're essentially telling the universe I want to attract situations where my physical and mental health are not respected. Whether those situations are relationships, jobs, or any other situation, they signify what you're putting out into the Universe.

# Chapter 4

## Attitude of Gratitude

So, what's the next step? How do we shift from lack luster careers, relationships, and habits to better build ourselves a happy healthy future? We create new neuropathways and it starts by being happy. Being happy has been proven to put your body in an alkaline state. No cancers or sickness can grow in this state. Being happy for what you have will give you an advantage over anything that can happen for you. Gratitude will rewire your subconscious brain. Your brain is just like a muscle group. When a certain pattern fires over and over, it eventually hardwires. It takes the extra neuropathways and shuts them down. Gratitude will help the old trauma pathways disintegrate so your subconscious mind doesn't run amuck.

Gratitude is the easiest way to start to give yourself new pathways again. Gratitude is like a super power. Gratitude shifts you to a different state of mind. It gives you the positive outlook on life that makes anything that happens a blessing. Gratitude creates miracles.

To demonstrate this notion, I was driving and my cruise control stopped working. I turned off the music, tuned in to my guides, and kept driving. I started giving my steering wheel buttons Reiki. I put in a symbol that I thought would help. I tried and tried to get it to work. Patient and knowing it might take some time, I just turned to gratitude to help me shift from being a little upset. I had another five hours to drive. About thirty minutes went by and I just said, I'm so happy and grateful that everything works in this van. I heard a voice say, "try the cruise control." I hit the button and it was back on, working again.

The way back on this trip I was driving and the cruise control stopped working again. I decided it was a good time to stop and take a break. I looked at the map on the phone to see how far I still had to drive only to realize I was going down the wrong road. Again, my guides were looking out for me. I started driving again and after I turned down the next major intersection to head back to the road I was supposed to be going down, my cruise control worked again. Talk about divine intervention? If I'm not paying attention, they help me pay attention by giving me signs. This connection has been strengthened through gratitude.

Gratitude in both of those situations removed me from suffering. Instead of being so focused on what was happening for me, I turned to gratitude to be thankful for the things that were going right. Anytime you use gratitude to remove yourself from the suffering state, you're choosing to be happy. Happiness will always be a choice. When you choose being happy, you're essentially telling the Universe, "This is what I want; this is my standard of living. Thank you for listening." Sometimes old neuropathways block us and happiness isn't the easiest choice. It can hide behind some old trauma still surfacing when you're triggered. When you realize that being sad, mad, distraught are also choices, you accept you're always making a choice. Happiness is the invisible door on the other side of awareness. It shows up when you can consciously look at how you're reacting. Painful trauma may still be blocking you from accepting that happiness is a choice; and if that's happening, then there's still work to do. This still happens to me in uncomfortable moments of my life. Sometimes it takes some serious honesty through self-inflection to reach this conclusion.

Anytime you think you don't have anything to be grateful for, then it's a good time to actually use comparison. Any other time I'd say never compare. But, compared to some lesser fortunate countries you could have a lot of amenities available to you. Places like Jamaica and Thailand have 2 or 3 wall huts, but they're very happy people. They don't have to compare that they have less. They see that they have a shelter, food, water, and sunshine and are a glowing happy people. Go travel to a second or third world country if you're from a first world country. This is the only time you should use comparison. Look at how much more you have available to you living in a first world country. You hit a switch the power goes on.

You turn a dial you have more heat. You go to the store and get whatever food you want from around the world. What isn't there to be grateful for? Stop focusing on what you're lacking and start focusing on what you have. You've been given so much!

I had so much at one point in my life: so much abundance, so much material wealth, so much to be grateful for. But I couldn't see it. I was blinded by consumerism and wanting more all the time. I had two rooms full of tools, and I could have started an electrical or carpentry business. But I couldn't see how much I should have been grateful for personally. After watching the documentary "Minimalism", I realized I was going about life all wrong. Why did I have so much stuff? It wasn't bringing me any joy at all. In fact, it was actually adding to my misery.

What are some exercises in gratitude you can practice? I have a gratitude journal where I write everything that I'm grateful for daily: everything from food, water, and shelter to the things I want to manifest and become. Everything is in the present tense whether I have it or not. By doing this, I'm showing the Universe that I'm grateful for my existence. The Universe then responds by giving me things to appreciate. Another exercise is I tell myself throughout the day as I'm receiving that I'm grateful for what I'm receiving. I thank everyone. Every time someone pours me a cup of coffee or lets me in a lane in traffic. I'm grateful. Even if they can't hear me or don't acknowledge my gratitude, I'm thankful.

When you go to a class and think you got nothing out of it, thank the instructor and peers. They honored you with their time and let you be part of their experience for the day. Even if no information was received, you got their time. Be grateful for everything. If someone has an emotional release around you, thank him or her. This person felt safe enough around you to let you in to his or her experience. Honor that. So many people shelter their emotions and don't release them in the moment. It's so hard to force that release at another time. They let you be part of their moment. Sometimes the most painful moments can be the most beautiful, honor that moment that you get to witness. Even if it's just a knowing look of compassion. The world is lacking in these moments being received fully. Don't be part of the problem.

Remember you always have a choice. Everything happens *for* you not *to* you. Sometimes things happen for you to show you where you need to shift. Sometimes things happen for you to demonstrate all the focus you give to your path is succeeding. Keep focusing on all the things you want in life. Pay no attention to anything seemingly going wrong. There's no such thing as something going wrong. You get to choose every day to be happy. You get to select where you focus your energy. Don't give that power away by focusing on the things you don't want. This is where you get to choose. Choose wisely.

# Chapter 5

## Clear the Clutter

After being completely honest with myself, I learned that I had some very severe anxiety. I hid it behind many substances, which manifested through the classic male pattern of aversion. I wasn't even willing to admit that there was a problem; I thought everyone went through life in borderline panic attack mode at any moment. I went over 30 years thinking that everyone felt that way. I was 28 years old before realizing that I even had depression. I thought it was normal to be sad all the time. But after seeing a psychologist and seeking help from doing an honest inventory, I tested in the top 99 percentile of anxiety. I don't think it even fully registered when the counselor told me. I think my ego was like "That's pretty rad!

I'm super unique. Yah, anxiety!" Talk about blinders in retrospect?!

We all have profound moments of self-realization. I have found that I'm so good at distracting myself I can become addicted to anything. Sometimes food, alcohol, or marijuana. I would binge on Netflix. I have very strong willpower, but the problem was I had to much stuff to distract me. In 2017, I went through a major spiritual shift throughout the process of going to physical rehabilitation for my wrist. In 2018, I sold almost every tool I owned, relinquished every piece of furniture except my bed. Within a year I moved my bed into my living room of my one and half story house and started using my house as a bachelor pad/Yoga studio. I'd successfully removed television, comfort and a lot of negative time-wasting habits from my life. Finally, I could start to focus of the root of the problem, me. Once I removed all of these things from my life, I had some very severe realizations that I was still very much an unhappy person.

Unable to distract myself with playing music during my wrist injury, I was inspired to take up other creative ventures as to avoid my minds constant negativity. I found I'm a gifted painter, drawer and eventually fully realized that I'm in fact a writer. Somehow in my brain, writing songs for over 10 years and poetry didn't count as me being a writer. This is a great example of *"don't listen to the lies"*.

I thus went back to my school years when I performed poorly in English classes because I really didn't care about what I was learning. Nonetheless, it's only recently that I've embraced the fact that I've always been a writer and always will be. This is the effect of the programming on our subconscious mind. We are taught to believe our teachers and they let me down. I also let myself down by accepting their words as my truth.

Once I removed the obstacles from my physical surroundings, I could then remove the obstacles from inside my mind. My external work was very strongly clouding my internal world. The more stuff I got rid of, the better I felt. Every time I sold twenty pounds worth of tools, I felt like I was physically carrying twenty pounds less. The more the rooms became empty, the more my mind became empty. See a pattern here? You need to empty your mind to be able to find your truth. If you're constantly cluttered by the teaching and lessons of everyone else how will you know what lessons you are giving yourself? Now this might not be as extreme for everyone. Only you'll know when you're still being distracted. You're the one who has to be honest with yourself there. You have to ask yourself once you have done a check in, am I using my time wisely? Is this break time, study time, or work time? All are acceptable. You need breaks so you can be more effective doing your work. You need to study so you know how to do your work. Everything is a fine balance.

The lessons you teach yourself are far more important than the stuff people tell you is important. I'm telling you: be discerning with all information that comes your way. Even this information. Some of it might seem like hokum to you. Good - then it is. But somewhere in this information you might find the key to the life changing event that jump starts your cataclysmic growth into becoming the best version of yourself possible.

Just being aware of having these realizations is a start your truth. Your truth is no one is going to say, "Frank: what a great guy he was great for owning all that stuff." People won't remember you for your possessions. Maybe your family will once you pass because they'll have to deal with your karmic burden? Don't put this burden on anyone. So be honest with yourself what do you own that actually brings you happiness.

The minimalism rule is: you hold it in your hand for 60 seconds. Does it bring you joy? Yes, keep it. No, get rid of it. It's very simple. You'll find as you grow, there will be things you originally said yes to that will change into a no. I held onto things for a year or two before realizing that keeping them was living in a lack mentality. Why did I need to keep a bunch of mechanic tools to lug around everywhere? This is manifesting that I don't have a reliable vehicle and I don't have the means to take care of my vehicle monetarily.

But enlightenment comes in waves and I'm a soul surfer. Always honor where you are at, at the time. I don't want to define enlightenment because it might give you an expectation of what it's supposed to be like. Instead, you'll know what it's like when you no longer feel the same. My version of changing won't be the same as yours. Your version of happiness won't be the same as mine. You might be completely content with having a ton of different personal items.

There's no comparison between two different people. As I said before, everyone on this Earth is completely unique with the gifts they can bring to the table, the gifts they can share with humanity. Becoming the best version of yourself opens up every gift you have available to you. Once you have a full realization on what gifts you have, then you can decide how you can use them to reach the most amount of people possible. We're supposed to want to help each other inherently. We need to rely on each other.

Would you have eaten today if it wasn't for someone else? No. I don't care if you're vegan and grow your own garden. Someone behind the scenes brought that water. Someone gave you the proper things to be able to store your food. Someone made your house. In a practical sense, no one is fully self-sufficient. I can make the off-grid home and completely make it self-sufficient, but I can't make the building supplies to make the home. So, don't believe that you can do it all yourself. The community raises the child.

If you haven't learned anything today, it's for a few reasons. The first reason is you aren't listening when people tell you things. The second reason is you aren't paying attention. You can learn a lot from watching. You learn from everyone. This is the mentality that you need to bring to the world with your gifts. What can you share with someone? You can be the building material that helps someone rebuild his or her life. You can be the emotional, physical or spiritual support that helps someone get out of a rut of depression, anxiety, or crippling debt.

When you know yourself, you can be yourself, and you can honor yourself fully. In honoring yourself fully, now you can help someone better. You can heal yourself better. Your life is in your control. You won't fall into the victim mentality. That vibration will no longer serve you. If you blame a circumstance or person, you'll be giving away your power, the power you need to fully take control of your life. Happiness is a choice. Will you be grateful for being able to get food and water today or will you be unhappy because things aren't going exactly as you have planned? You need to look past the illusion of consumerism.

When you use victim mentality, you tell the Universe, "I want to be a victim." You don't get what you want; you get what you are. You must use your conscious awareness to always be aware of what you're saying. When you say, "I'm successful and happy," the Universe will give you success and more reasons to be happy. Always be aware of what you're saying. Always be aware of who you're saying it to as well. If you have a relationship where all you do is get together and complain then, that isn't a healthy relationship. You get to choose. When you choose a relationship that falls under that pattern, you're telling the Universe, "I'm not worthy of a better, healthier relationship."

# Chapter 6

## Society's Two Monsters

Society has created two huge monsters that roam around and wreak havoc on whoever lets them in their lives. What or who are these monsters? The first monster is objectivity through materialism. Objectivity is desire to own, desire to buy, and accumulate everything. I've fallen victim to this distraction. Consumerism dictates how we live our lives. They study very close the human psyche and determine the next best way to sell the thing. The thing is the product you need to buy. They study us with great precision and incorporate more and more ways to get easy access to all of our information which generates the marketing behind all of this. Every 8 minutes, the next new fad or gadget will come out and you won't be cool unless you have it.

Do you think aboriginal people around the world a thousand years ago wanted the new feather or medicine pot? No, I don't think so either. As a society, they blind us with objectivity to make the money machine keep going and going. Don't feed this machine with your money. It's not an ATM; in sum, it's a way to drain you of your resources. Once you're drained of your resources, then you have to suffer. This breeds the discontent that lives in the hearts of so many would be great achievers in education and most importantly happiness. Do you really need the shiniest new thing? I can guarantee you don't.

The second monster society has created is debt. This idea of non-stop cash at any moment. Three credit cards are being sent to you as we speak! This is a dangerous blinder society has created. As a result, one monster feeds the other, and they both grow to be big and strong. These monsters' team up and destroy your spirit. We aren't meant to overconsume. Think if you had to eat money, would you be fat? Some people are fat with money/power/coveting or even knowledge. Society wants you to be greedy. Through the design of the lack mentality, you get mental illness. Mental illness is what keeps that monster fed. Think of the classic phrases people and society will tell you:

- You can always make more money!
- Be the first person to have the thing.
- Everyone will be jealous of you!
- Don't you want to keep in communication with your friends and family?
- You'll be more attractive with a new car.
- You can buy whatever you want.
- Don't you want to be cool?
- Everyone's doing it.
- Everyone has the new thing.
- What will the neighbors think?

Let's be really clear: all of these phrases and I'm sure the ten thousand other ones I'm missing, reflect society's way of being a bully. Society is a bully: and if you get raised by a bully, you either become one yourself and/or become a victim. Stop being a victim to anyone or any circumstance. Your will-power has to be greater. Your will-power is your truth. Do I need a new TV? Do I need a TV at all?

I was sitting with my Grandma a few years ago and she turned to me and said, "Do you like the program that we're watching?" I replied, "I think it's fine. I'm happy watching anything. I'm happy just to be sitting on a couch." She suggested, "I can change it you want." I insisted, "*No,* you watch whatever you want to watch." She then asked me, "What do you do in your free time." I admitted, "I read, I write, I meditate, I do Yoga, I play music, and I enjoy cooking." She inquired, "You don't have a TV?" I said, "No." She literally put her fist to the side of her head and did the whole "my brain is exploding" hand gesture.

First off, how did an 83-year-old lady know that gesture? Secondly, she's been in the whole picture of the technological forefront of the evolution of the television. How can someone who grew up in Europe poor, being considered rich if you had a radio when you were young, not see how someone can so easily spend one's time without this advanced technology? People soon forget the things they had. They become so blinded by how easy it is to go buy the next shiny new thing, they forget that in their lifetime just being able to have music readily available was and is miraculous. In my life, the computer changed so rapidly and the advancements of the internet made whatever music I wanted readily available. I didn't have to wait to buy the CD, since I could just download it whenever.

This readily available stuff has made people impatient. An album is released at midnight. Then if your phone buffers a bit at 12:01, everyone goes bonkers! They lose it. I've such fast-wireless internet I want it now. I'm sorry - if you can't wait a day or 30 minutes for a song or the new Smartphone, then you really need to do self-inventory. You really need to grasp the idea of gratitude. Buddha says if you're busy, then you should meditate for 20 minutes a day. But if you're really busy, you should meditate for an hour. There's great wisdom in that lesson. Everyone gets so blinded by consumerism, it dictates how we spend our time, where we spend our money, what drives us, and how to make more money so we can buy that shiny new thing. This rapid consumerism breeds impatience. This is insanity, complete and utter insanity.

When we stop feeding the one monster, it stops feeding the other. Life is supposed to be very simple. We make it so complex by believing all of the things we're told that we should be doing and not doing. But if you weren't told any of that, what would you be really doing? Aspiring to watch the next season of *Big Brother*? I don't even know if that show is still on. But that isn't an extreme example of putting the priority of entertainment before your health? Your health is so much more than the physical vessel. We're far more intricate than Western science can comprehend at this moment in time.

So many times, numerous people have told me they're sick. I ask them what they eat. I hear the same thing: I eat this and this other thing that's made from processed foods. I ask them why they can't make meals from whole foods? Again, I receive the same answers repeatedly. They allege,

"I don't have time." Meanwhile they're watching TV nonstop. This is priority problem. Your priorities are a direct reflection of your willpower and self-love. What you consume will help you or consume you.

Science is finally discovering that people can absorb each other's energy. Have you ever been sitting in a room and had someone really negative or positive walk in and felt a shift in the energy? I'm sure you have. I believe people used to be way more attuned to these energies we carry. I think people used to be a lot happier so feeling this pull of the opposite side of the magnet of the negative person wasn't so prevalent. Why did we not have problems like depression being a huge problem in the past? I believe people were less distracted. We were less distracted by technology. We were less distracted by shiny things, less distracted by light pollution, less distracted by noise pollution. We were less distracted in every way. Just think: 100 years ago, power was a barely accessible thing. Radios weren't in every household. Barely anyone could just jump in a car and drive to the supermarket. Supermarkets didn't carry readily available food from around the world twenty-four hours a day.

Again, the global accessibility now has let the monster of consumerism run amuck on our lives. Like who really needs food at 3:30AM? 100 years ago, people didn't have fridges. They'd be sleeping because they wouldn't have power. There wouldn't be light pollution from streetlights. People wouldn't be driving around creating other noise pollution. The list goes on. All of these distractions are affecting our health in every way. We're so over saturated with the amount of stuff available to our fingertips at any given time that we've lost the ability to be happy just to be warm and fed.

I'm not suggesting that we should completely abolish all the technology that has made our lives so easy and amazing. However, we need to be super grateful for being able to have all of these things. Every time you call your friend on the other side of the globe through a video-chat, you should be in admiration of the miracle that's happening. Without technology we wouldn't be so connected. But it's also the thing that's blinding us from actually having the real connection. It's so amazing to be able to talk to anyone any time you want.

The real interaction between the human vessels is the miracle we're all ignoring. When you sit with someone and have a real conversation. I'm talking *real* conversation. When you authentically talk about your passions and goals, you emit a high frequency energy into that conversation. That feeling isn't so easily transmitted like a television signal. It's not like making a phone call. When someone cares to hear what you have to say, you've truly been received. This is the feeling that's very important to our souls. We're just like a radio station. If a radio station had no listeners, would it go out of business? Probably. They have to transmit and being received is just as important as their transmission. We human beings are exactly the same. If you're in a relationship where the other person doesn't value or care about what you're saying, you're literally wasting your energy. You just pump energy into the streetlights of your internal self where no one goes walking. So, finding someone to receive you is important for your healing it's vital for your soul. Psychologists know this. Most of them talk to other psychologists. Let's take Abraham Maslow, who wrote Maslow's Hierarchy of Needs. He outlines the need for community with the second highest point on his pyramid, Esteem. Esteem is your social needs. We all need community to self-actualize. In his findings, experts in that respected field of psychology deem it's necessary for the mental body to function properly. They know that without their body functioning properly, they won't be able to help others in an effective way.

I believe the community feeling was way stronger everywhere in the world. If you go to countries that are less economically fortunate, they still have these communities. They still have a high regard for the importance of happiness. They support each other, talk, communicate through touch, and exude emotions. This is why family values are very important. This is why these communities regard their women as the highest form of humanity. The mother is the giver of life. The mother is the compassionate person in the family and community. This is the most amazing miracle. Science shows this and reinforces it through mirrored neurons. Mirrored neurons are a neuron that fires when an animal acts and when an animal observes the same action performed by another. The neuron functions as a mirror from the behavior of the others, as I'm sure you've encountered and witnessed this. When you enter a room full of love and appreciation, you give love and appreciation if not just feeling loved and appreciated. When you witness someone getting hurt and you feel the pain, this is the mirrored neurons firing away.

# Chapter 7

## Embrace the Miracles

Our miracles in life are the "things" we often regard such as gaining wealth or achieving a goal. On the other hand, the true miracles are the things that have been happening for thousands, if not millions, of years. Consciousness is a miracle: the ability to hone our thoughts into complex ideas and grow those ideas into helping people through our technology. This is a true miracle.

At one point it was an amazing miracle to have a car. Now we automatically just jump in this automobile and drive. When we take for granted the things that were once miracles, since they become expectations. You get mad when your car doesn't start, did you proactively take care of it? Did something unforeseen happen? What's the real reason behind your distaste for the car not starting? Is it because you have to be somewhere on time? Is this because society has created this illusion of time? At 9:01 you're in trouble now. Thus, inducing panic and anxiety. This isn't a healthy way to live. Do yourself a favor if you get so easily troubled by time, wake up early. If you get anxious from being late, a few things might be happening to you. You might be wanting to be in control of the situation. You might be being controlled by the situation. Either one of those things will cause dis-ease. Let go of control! Let go of being controlled. If you can't make it to work on time ever and getting up 15 minutes earlier still isn't solving the problem, maybe the problem is you don't want to be there?

To offer a personal context, I used to get to my one job exactly on time. I'd never get there early. The problem was they had the expectation that you had to be early or you were late. You started work at 8, so if you weren't there by 7:45, you weren't somehow ready. This was the employer's way of manufacturing more of my time. Well, it didn't work. It has harnessed resentment for being used for my time. No matter what I did, I'd never make it early. I'd wake up fifteen minutes earlier, and I'd even wake up thirty minutes earlier. It was not until years later that I realized I can't be constrained by a specific time doing something I don't want to do. Give me plus or minus fifteen min and I'll hit that time window. But if I woke up earlier, I'd find more distractions. Now I had time to eat a better breakfast. So, it took longer and I made it to work at the same exact time as before. Then I'd eat a better breakfast and start watching a program on Netflix. Boom, I'd barely make it to work on time. The problem wasn't the amount of time I needed to be up before going to work. The problem was the expectation. The problem was the distraction I created to avoid dealing with the expectation.

I had such a hard time as a supervisor telling people what to do. It was "like, hey man, I know this job really sucks and I personally hate this aspect of the particular task - do you think you would want to do it?" Some of them would say no. Then I'd have to do it. But that's what leadership is: keeping people happy. Sometimes I couldn't do it and they'd have to, but stepping up and doing it every once and a while shows that it's both capable of being done and you respect that they aren't expected to do it all as the lower level employee.

My point of all of this is you should find an employer who aligns with the fact that life isn't perfect. If he or she has crazy expectations of you that you cannot meet, then you find someone who doesn't. The more you accept being controlled, the more the Universe is going to control you. As soon as you hold yourself strong in your power, you tell the Universe that I'm in control of my destiny. I may not be in control of every circumstance of things that happen for me, but my direction, goals, and values are my best interest. When you stop settling, you won't have to settle. The Universe will respond. The powers that be will see you as your own guiding force and step clearly out of the freight train's way.

The higher love for yourself will dictate how you're to be treated. When you choose yourself, you'll gain more options to choose yourself. The Universe will throw old scenarios back at you to see if you really want to choose yourself or take the easy path. When you stop the comparison mindset, you'll realize that you're so unique, so there's no beneficial reason for you to ever compare yourself to others. We're snowflakes: everyone has one's own pattern, unique brilliance, individual beauty, and diverse shapes. What happens when a snowflake touches the ground on a warming day? It melts. It turns into a puddle and melds with the other snowflakes. Stay a snowflake. Don't touch the proverbial ground that society has created. Don't let society melt you. Stay unique: it's, in that beautiful uniqueness that illuminates the qualities of your life. In those qualities you can be so perfect just for yourself. You'll never be perfect for someone else. Release the idea of that crazy notion. Even if they think in the time this person is perfect for me. You won't stay the same and eventually you won't be perfect for them anymore. Be wary of people who deem you as perfect. They aren't seeing life clearly. You only need to be perfect for yourself. Part of being perfect is embracing that you aren't perfect. Here lies a paradox. When you accept yourself as the person you are, you never need to be perfect, and that's what perfection is. Perfection is acceptance.

# chapter 8

## Being an Empath

The new age community is going to be unhappy with me after this chapter. I say, "Let them." You deserve to know what is really going on. You deserve to know about the synchronicities that have happened to you and what the real reasons they happened. Some people might find this whole chapter too fantastical to believe. Good, don't believe it. It really does no harm to me. We aren't living in a day and age where I'm to be burned at the stake. So, you get to decide if you believe this one hundred percent or call this chapter "The chapter of lies." It really makes no difference to me. You'll only get something out of it by believing it.

Now I'm sure you have heard the term "empath" being thrown around a lot. Maybe you're new to the word? Maybe new to the idea of what an empath really is? I believe everyone is an empath. There isn't someone walking around in a human vessel who isn't an empath. I think the true sensitive empaths are the ones that embrace it. The true empaths embrace their sensitivities as a super power by not shutting them out. The true empaths will cry because they're not scared of showing their emotions.

So, what's an empath exactly? What does the word mean? The generalized meaning of an empath is someone who feels others emotions. This is a very general statement. On an electrical level, we all sense each other's emotions. Remember how I mentioned mirrored neurons before? Our emotional brain is what's mirroring the feelings that make you an empath. When you're observing someone's emotions, you might also be feeling them and maybe even showing the same emotions. This will be true for almost everyone, unless you're on the high end of the spectrum for narcissistic personality disorder, or a sociopath. If you're either one of those, you might be able to observe the emotions, but not feel them. A true-to-their-self empath will have way more gifts than that when he or she really tunes in and embraces their gifts. An empath is someone in-touch with one's sensitivity and then embraces this sensitivity to intuit the needs of everyone around them. I'd say it's something they all use for good, but I also think that every narcissist is also an empath. They have to be too-- they intuit people's needs so well that they can manipulate and take advantage of others. What are the powers of the empaths? And how exactly do they work? I asked my guides to help me channel the answers.

In brief, I believe there are the five Clair abilities: Clairvoyance, Claircognizance, Clairsentience, Clairscense, and Clairaudience. Each one is a super power that you have one or all of depending on how sensitive you really are. So, I'm here to set the record straight: you're all super heroes waiting to discover your secret abilities. The easiest way to unlock these gifts is to stop denying that they don't exist. In high school I'd talk to and see spirits. I was very afraid that others would make fun of me. I didn't tell more than a few people of what I saw, I don't know if anyone other than my brother knew that I could talk to spirits not just see them. Because I denied myself this wonderful gift, I stopped seeing spirits and lost the ability to communicate with them. Once I again embraced it, it came back. But had I honed this gift from a young age, I would've been able to better use it to help people. Let's talk about each Clair and see if it rings any bells, or if you just know that they're "going off" (that will make sense by the end of this chapter).

I'm sure at this point you all have heard of Clairvoyance. Clairvoyance is also called and known as "clear sight." Clairvoyance is the ability to see things beyond the normal physical spectrum of the human eyesight. Everyone is clairvoyant. When you're a kid you have "imaginary friends" and your teachers or family members will tell you to stop talking to that person since he or she isn't really there. They'll allege that you're just making things up. This is how we lose a lot of Clairvoyance. We're told as kids that parents and adults are right and we should listen to them. So, we do. This is a huge problem in the development of this gift. What you're seeing in your third eye is energy, but we're so sensitive to seeing this energy that when we're in a pure state, it's possible to see as a real physical manifestation. A lot of mediums embrace and use this as one of their gifts of communication with spirits from different dimensions. On a scientific level, dimensions are just different frequencies. Some see higher frequencies; some see lower frequencies. I believe some see them all. This is solely dependent on how profoundly Clairvoyant you really are. What are you seeing if you're Clairvoyant? Some people will see a void almost like a shadow. Some people see a translucent figure. These are examples of seeing a spirit or ghost. Some Clairvoyants will see colors and lights around people or even see a light by itself. This is an example of seeing an aura or guide or orb or even an angel. What people see will vary from person to person. Some see all of it.

The second Clair I mentioned is Claircognizance. Claircognizance is also known as "clear knowing." I'm very Claircognizant. Sometimes you might have this knowing that something is going to happen and then it does. Embrace this knowing and thank the Universe for it. Claircognizance is a powerful lie detector. It can help let you know what's right and wrong. This gift isn't described as a sound or feeling. When you ask a question and hear nothing but just know the answer, that's Claircognizance. Have you ever known information about a particular subject and never done any research on that subject? This has happened to me so many times in my life. Before I knew it had a name, I'd just tell people I know. Many times, people would ask. "Yah, but how do you know?" I'd just say "I don't know how I know, but I just know." Claircognizance can work for information in the past or things that haven't even happened yet in the future. It's a powerful tool fortune teller use. Some use Clairvoyance to see the future some use Claircognizance to know the future. Either seeing or knowing, if your vessel is clean and in tune, this gift can be very accurate. Some will talk of Clairtangency. It is described as knowing the history of the item through touch. I believe that it is Claircognizance telling you by touching the item. By touching the item, you become in-tune with it more intimately. You can believe either or both.

The next Clair is probably the most prevalent in people. It's Clairsentience, also known as "clear feeling." I think this one is so prevalent because we're such strong electrical devices. Our hearts are the strongest chakra, since the heart produces a lot more electrical magnetic force than any other pump or chakra in our body. When you go to a feel-good concert and everyone is happy, you can be sober and it can feel like ecstasy. Why is that? We're effectively absorbing the collective feeling of everyone's hearts around us. This is why a lot of musicians intuitively will ask the audience to come closer to the stage. When people are closer, they get to feel their energy from the music. When they feel their energy, they feel better and perform better. When you're in a conflict, you can cut the tension with a knife. How else are we feeling that? Where else would that feeling come from but our energetic body tuning in with our physical and mental bodies? If you cannot believe this, then you're in huge denial. Everyone has felt this. I have felt them feel it! When this gift is sensitive you can feel exactly what is going on in someone's body. When you train in Reiki and are devoted to healing others, this gift knows exactly when to amplify.

You can tune in to the exact spot of a dis-ease on someone's body. It's truly magical and there are no words to describe it other than miraculous.

The next Clair I mentioned is Clairscense. This is also known as "clear smelling." Clear smelling is exactly is as it sounds. Sometimes a spirit will carry a scent with them that will be a representation of something they used to do in the physical life. I've had people talk about I smell this exact perfume that their grandmother used to wear. Other times I've heard people talk about a specific tobacco or baking. Whatever the scenario is, they smell something that isn't manifested in the physical realm but in one form of an energetic frequency aligned with smell. I've even heard about mediums using this to describe that exact scent from a family member to a client. It can be the evidence needed sometimes to the client that the psychic is in fact not just making things up. I've experienced Clairscense a few times, and it has confused me as much as the person receiving it. I've often looked for the physical evidence of the smell to no avail. Others might mention Clairgustance which is described as "clear tasting."

But as we all know our smell and taste are in direct correlation. I believe that that if you possess Clairscense you probably have witnessed Clairgustance as well. But I do not believe it to be a main Clair.

The last Clair is called Clairaudience. It's known as "clear hearing." This is what a lot of people have that get misdiagnosed. I'm hearing things. Ok, let's get this straight jacket on you, you're a crazy person. The problem is the medications they give the "patient" actually clog up the pineal gland and the voices stop. So, the psychiatrist goes see the meds are working! Wrong. You've untuned someone with amazing gifts by not understanding their spiritual body is alive and needs some tuning and some help. A lot of people have heard voices. In fact, I used to hear voices all the time when I was younger. There are many people who will think they hear voices but in reality, it's Claircognizance. So effectively they're listening to their brain tell them instead of their ears. This takes some real fine tuning to know the difference, especially if you don't know that there is a difference between the two.

I only mention all the Clairs' because being in tune with them will really help you see, know, feel, smell, or hear the messages you are missing. Those signals are messages of guidance that will help you greatly on your path to both healing yourself and helping others heal. Everyone has all of these gifts. You might be stronger in two or three over the others. This is no different than the fact that everyone has a different type of body. You could be lean, big, tall, or short. We're all different. I'm certain the gifts you've been given is part of both your soul path and your physical genetics.

So, which of these gifts resonates with you? What speaks to you? These gifts are in all of us. They only become available by tuning into them. You have to believe that you're gifted. If you shut them out and say they aren't real they will shut down and not work properly. Don't listen to someone if they tell you it isn't real. He or she is just embracing what one has learned. Modern day society doesn't want you to have these gifts. Because they're not widely accepted, and they are not fully understood. Be wary of who you tell.

# Chapter 9

## Removing Labels

What's the mighty battle of good versus bad? Good and bad are a few labels that have been created to hold you back. Remember two things. The first reality is there is no good. The second truth is there is no bad. When someone tells you "oh do this it is very good", or "do not do this other thing it is very bad," don't believe them. They're society's snake oil salesmen and saleswomen.

I'm sure you've heard this during commercials. Our product is the best on the market. So, what's the problem with this label? When you create the label of good for a place, situation, thing, or person you create an expectation. With that expectation, you then formulate the idea that everything that's good has gone a certain way. I'll give you an example. You only want an Audi car. You've read all the reviews and, in your mind, they're the best cars on the market. Now when you go to purchase the car you realize that they are very expensive. Now you've created some suffering from not being able to afford to buy the Audi. Without knowing it you have made your life harder. You create this idea that this is the only car I want and now I cannot be happy without it. How will you live your life without this specific car? Instead, you can be grateful to be able to buy any car. I'm not saying don't buy the car you want. I'm suggesting, don't be so attached to the idea of the car you want that it causes you to suffer.

Let's think of another example. Say you have this list of the perfect attributes of a person you want to attract. Now this list is extensive and very specific. By following this list, you could be looking past all of the main things you need in a relationship. Sure, if you have love, acceptance, guidance, and reciprocity, it'd be a good list. But when you're seeking someone to spend your life with, a partner isn't a bunch of groceries. When you create these lists, you're deciding a expectation for what you want him or her to be like in your mind. When the person changes 2 days later to 5 years later, you're going to be dis-eased. You will say you were like this before why did you change. Change is the nature of life. Without change we cannot grow. Everything in life and nature changes, it shifts to being something different. When you seek out a partner to be with in life, you should be attracted to one's spirit.

I was saying at the start of this book, people aren't magnets. Like attracts like. So, if you attract someone and you want to change something about them that means you still want to change something about yourself. At that point there are two ways you can go with life: first, you can divinely accept yourself as whole. The second way is to not enter a relationship at that time because the Mirror Paradox is telling you, "I am not comfortable with myself right now. I couldn't possibly be comfortable with someone else." You need to remove yourself gracefully from the relationship and start working on healing yourself. If you're bleeding and you put on a brand-new white shirt, what will happen to the shirt? You'll bleed all over it. You must clean the wound and let it heal before you cover it with the material you want to have in your life. Your relationships are like really nice clothing. You must take care of them. You must be clean in thoughts and actions as to not stain the relationship.

So, give up the idea of good since you create an expectation that will lead you into suffering. Every time things aren't good; you'll think this is bad. If this is bad, I must suffer. Stop expecting everything to be good. How can everything be good all the time? We're given a situation, which can just be a normal situation. Then we ruin it with a label. We ruin the situation with an expectation. If you want to say things are going great for me right now. Say it a way that doesn't impose the things to be going great because of the particular situation. No matter what, things are going great because I chose not to be emotionally dictated by anything. Whatever happens to me, things are going perfect. This is exactly as it's supposed to be right now. In this exact moment, perfect.

Now let's talk about the label of bad. When we label things as bad, we're really creating a label of "I do not want that." When it comes to the Law of Attraction, that simply means the language of vibration, I want that. Vibration does not know don't, and can't. So, when we label things bad, we're silently manifesting the things that we don't want to happen to occur to us. This can be dangerous to our health in a few ways. The first way is we're again creating an expectation. When we don't get what we want, we then harbor more dis-ease. You essentially set yourself up for failure. Do yourself a favor and don't worry about what you don't want. The second way its causes dis-ease is that it's a huge waste of your time. If you sat there and labeled all the things you didn't want and are trying to avoid, you'd waste half your day. Use your time wisely. We're infinite beings of potential with finite amounts of time.

Bad is a label that doesn't serve you anymore. It's like when you find out you're lactose intolerant. You don't drink milk anymore. I'm letting you know you're both good and bad intolerant. These labels won't help you anymore. It's time to shed them and the other stigmas society has created to give you a better outlook on life.

Give yourself a code of conduct, but realize if someone strays from your code of conduct, they aren't bad people. They have to have different views. If everyone thought and felt the same about everything; there'd be one kind of house, one car company. Follow your own code. When people follow their own code, it's awesome. Some people might want to take some of your ideals and use them for their own. Cool, let them. You might meet an inspiring person and change your code after that. Do it. We change every second, day, month, and year. Embrace it.

When we follow the close dualities of good and bad, we create a small box that we want to live in. Instead, we could be looking at the whole world. If you tell yourself, "I only want friends from this nationality." You could be cutting off the information stream that would bring you to that higher level of awareness. When you create a vision of only wanting the most expensive car, you could be then feeding society's monsters again. Live within your means. Let's stay humble in everything we do. If you can't afford an Audi right now, then either save up for one or don't buy one.

Too many people blame others for their problems. Oh, this girl didn't like me because I wasn't exactly fulfilling her expectations. Cool, that's awesome. You weren't meant to be and someone that could see you and accept you for who you are can now come along. Don't play the "I am going to change them" game. Once they start doing this, then we can get married. Either accept them and stay or accept them and move on. When we remove these labels, we effectively free ourselves from suffering.

# Chapter 10

## Radical Acceptance

There's a powerful way you can change your life. Acceptance. Radical acceptance is accepting everything that's happening. Radical acceptance is from Dialectal Behavioral Therapy. It is defined as "complete and total acceptance that permeates through every part of your being." We can acknowledge that our current circumstance cannot be changed unless we are willing to accept it. Radical acceptance isn't about denying the emotions either. Accept that you might get happy, mad or sad in the situation. This doesn't mean you have to agree with what has happened. By accepting what has happened, you get remove yourself from being a victim. When you remove the victimhood mentality, you don't have to dwell on why the situation has occurred. You can accept the situation that's happened. You can also accept that you might want to change so these situations don't happen anymore. When you use radical acceptance, you can turn any situation into "Ok, now what am I going to do about this situation," instead of denying the reality of the situation. You release the need to be disheartened in life.

Let's look at troubleshooting. The first step to solving a problem is acknowledging that the problem exists. Every one that has ever used this troubleshooting logic is practicing radical acceptance. Let's say you're going to fix a light in a house. The first step is trying the light. Even though the light had been tested by someone else before you were called to fix the light, before you got there, the light not working wasn't your reality. You test the light and it's not working. Now you can start looking into why it's not working because you've established that there is a problem. You've accepted that there is something to fix. Do you get upset when the light doesn't work? Of course not. You were called there to fix it.  Acknowledging the problem is the same thing as seeing the pattern of disharmony in our lives. If you're in an abusive situation and you cannot acknowledge that there's something wrong, what are the chances of you getting out of that situation?

When your car breaks down, you're like, "Cool. No big deal, I could use a good walk." When your girlfriend breaks up with you, you can say, "Amazing, that means we weren't meant to be and the Universe will send someone else along." Radical acceptance will free you from being hurt. It is the silver lining. It sounds crazy to not be a little annoyed when either of those things happens. But what's crazy is letting something beyond your control ruin your hour, day, month, or year. You don't need to be controlled by your emotions, but that doesn't mean you won't feel them either.

So, if your dad comes to you and says, "I don't know why you don't eat meat, I don't understand how you survive!". Don't get upset. Accept the fact that he doesn't understand. He doesn't need to understand. There's a fine line in this, though. I'm not saying accept abuse from anyone. That isn't radical acceptance: that's abuse. Walk away from people calling you down. You can accept that they don't understand or have the compassion that you have. But when you stick around and get abused, that shouldn't be confused with you accepting yourself. Accepting the way that you're treated doesn't mean absorbing the way you're treated. Walk away.

Use both radical acceptance and compassion to illuminate your path. If someone told me, "Frank, you're a horrible guy," I'd say, "I accept your opinion; I don't believe it, but I do accept it. Thank you". Now that person has shown me that I don't need him or her in my life. I can accept that. When you remove codependent tendencies to need someone in your life, you can have the best time just being alone. Don't get emotionally attached to them not liking or liking you. Both are dangerous. You're the only one that needs to like you.

When we practice acceptance, we can remove the expectations from our lives, we can remove dis-ease from our hearts, bodies, and minds. When we practice acceptance, we can remove ourselves from suffering. Why would we want to suffer? We reside in a time when we can get food any hour of the day. We can stimulate our minds and thoughts whenever we want. This is the golden age of being so free. We can travel wherever we want in the world. Why would we want to suffer? When we accept, we remove the part of us that would attach to the suffering. If you lock yourself out of your house, maybe it's because ◆ you needed a walk. If you want, you can accept everything as a miracle. When you expect miracles, you'll get miracles!

Let me give you an example. I bought a van and after purchasing it I realized the one door didn't fully work. I couldn't lock it from the outside and the back handle didn't work very well. At the time I got a little upset but I wasn't angry. I found if I jiggled it just right, I could still get in but in a way that you'd still think the door was locked. So, I never really locked it after that, it was like a secret way to get into my van. Two weeks ago, I went to work and when I went to get my key out of my ignition it wouldn't come out. So naturally I was a little upset. I was worried about it for a few days but I happened to have an extra key with me the day it happened, so I was able to lock my van and secure my things.

One week ago, I was going to get a computer and I locked my room at the Airbnb that I am staying at. This was at 10 am. So, I was a little upset, but I realized it was happening to stop me from buying the computer. I contacted the Airbnb manager of my place and asked her about another key to get into my room. She said she had a key but she was busy and wouldn't be able to bring it until 7:00 at night. I needed to leave for work at 5:30 at night. So, this was a problem, because I needed different clothing from my room for work. So, I asked her if I could come get the key. Had I been upset about the door on my van not working; I would have gotten it fixed. Had I been upset about my key being stuck in the ignition; I would have had it repaired. But because I could get into my van and start my van, I could go get my key so I could get into my room to get to work on time. All of these things which seemingly could have upset me were miracles in disguise. Had I got mad about them; I would have later realized that these were things happening for me not to me.

I have an affirmation that I say all the time: "The Universe is always looking out for me." So, whether that affirmation was protecting my van or protecting me or both, it responded in kind. Life isn't out to get you, unless you think it is. At that point it's not life getting you: it's you getting yourself. You create the disharmony through the belief system you create for yourself. Now you can create a new one! If something isn't working in life, it's a good sign. It's either time to change your awareness to the situation or change the situation. Don't fall into the victim role where you say you have no choice.

I'm just supposed to be unhappy right now. That's a load of crap. If you're in the mindset that you're supposed to be unhappy and wondering why things aren't changing, it's because you're not changing your mindset. Your mindset will change your outcome. When you change your mindset, you change your results. If you constantly think, "I am not good enough to do this," you'll believe it. Don't tell the Universe or anyone else you aren't good enough. You *are* good enough, and you deserve to be happy. Everything you put out you will get back. Don't convince yourself or anyone else you don't deserve your basic needs. It's essential for your basic needs to include your happiness.

# Chapter 11

## Survival

You need some basic things to survive and many cultures embrace and inherently know this. You need food, water, shelter, air, and love. Many people would say you really only need food water and shelter to survive. A lot of people aren't looking at the big picture. You can go a few weeks without food. You can go a few days without water. You can go at best 10 minutes without air. But why do we need love? And what love am I describing? I'm not talking about romantic love. You need connection and community to survive. Like I was stating before you can't be fully self-sufficient. You need some emotional connections to feed your spirit. You'll become dull, and emotionally dead without the proper connections.

Why are these connections so important to your human survival? Because the survival of the human being has gone way beyond what they've taught us in school. Our survival isn't highly regarded as taking care of the emotional body nearly as much as it is taking care of the physical body. Sure, when we take care of the body the body takes care of the mind. To a certain extent, this is very true. But when you don't actively take care of the mind, the mind cannot take care of the body. Everything needs to be in balance in your life.

If you do a huge physical detox on processed food then the next day go to celebrate by having a beer, you're not taking care of the body. If you do a huge detox on the mind and body by going to Yoga and then have a beer at the end of the class, you're toxifying your system making all of the progress you may have had null and void. I'm not saying never have that drink or never eat a bad thing again after doing a fast or exercise. But you have to be honest with yourself as to what it is you were trying to get out of your system. If you wanted it out of your system so bad that you were willing to fast for two days to clear your physical pathways, then how much willpower are you exercising by consuming it right away again? Your will has to be strong. This is where warrior mentality kicks in. We have this innate warrior within us ready to fight. We no longer have to physically engage in combat in regular day occurrences. But this warrior should not be lying dormant. This warrior is your will power that you get to harness anytime you choose you over a substance, situation, or person.

You have to able to choose will over desire. Desires are still healthy when you consume them in moderation. A lot of people who study nutrition know that seventy percent of the serotonin in your body is created in the gut from the healthy food you consume. Thirty percent of the serotonin you create is in the brain. This thirty percent is from you eating the donut when you want to. This doesn't mean you can eat one hundred donuts and make enough serotonin to survive. No, this means if you consume what you want and what you need in a healthy balance, then you'll have a healthy balance of serotonin. That same analogy can be used for your entire body.

Let's talk about consumption. Like I said before, you need food, water, shelter, air and love to survive. Of which of those five necessities are you consuming something? I'd say four of them have you consuming something in which keeps you alive. When I say I alive, I don't mean malnourished and unhappy. I mean thriving. There are two choices in life, either consume healthy things, or be consumed by unhealthy things. You decide.

You need food like I was talking about formerly. Healthy food nourishes your physical body to be able to perform at a happy level. When you consume good food, you feel good. When you consume water, it helps cleanse and keep your organs and muscles pure from holding onto any toxins. The water you drink is as important as the food you eat if not more important. It's common knowledge that we would survive for weeks without food and days without water. Water-- it's my red-hot sauce, I put that shit on everything! All jokes aside, it's crucial for our physical bodies. Not just our internal bodies but water cleanses us from the outside too. If we don't clean ourselves, we're showing the world we want to attract unclean relationships.

I don't think I need to rant about air. It's also common knowledge that you'd be brain dead ten minutes into not getting enough air. But we can talk about smoking? When you ingest toxins into your system, you're telling the Universe, "I am willing to ingest toxins." You create a manifestation platform for other things toxic. Be honest with yourself: it's toxic. Your will is directly attached to your self-love. So as long as you keep making the excuses that "oh, but addiction is so hard and I can't quit I'll do it next year," you're telling the addiction that it has more power than you do. Essentially you give your power away. If addiction is a problem, do yourself a favor. Find something that helps you build your willpower. Start jogging or running, do a fast once a month or intermittent fast a few times a week, and/or wake up early and do Yoga. This will change your brain to the warrior mentality. You're now creating this badass that's inside of you that chooses you. Take small steps and embrace them when you are successful. Don't believe that you need something else to mask the substance that you're trying to detox. If you start drinking unhealthy amounts of coffee to quit smoking then you are still being unhealthy. I will say it again- your will is directly connected to your self-love.

When it comes to the balance of handling your addictions, your willpower directly affects your physical, mental, and spiritual bodies. I say bodies because they're not the same bodies. We have multiple bodies sharing one vessel all working in harmony. Any one of those bodies can be out of alignment and impact the other one or all of them. By embracing your willpower and not giving in to any addictions, you can effectively balance the energy between these bodies. What happens when energy builds up and we can't release it? It manifests as a mental or physical injury. So, when you have a small victory with your willpower, celebrate it and embrace it. Tell yourself I did this because I'm a warrior! When you build that willpower, you build that self-love. That self-love is so important. Without it, you'll attract situations that will hurt, and show you that you don't properly love yourself.

Earlier in my life I came to the conclusion that I've never actually fully experienced love. I've experienced passion, lust, jealousy, and a mix if all the other emotions. But never have I actually been in love. How could I? I was so brainwashed into believing what I thought love was. I wasn't even close.

I'm going to give you an example. Love is like a flower. You love this flower so much you water it and give it shade if it's too hot out. If you want your flower to continue to grow, you'll leave it planted. You go to work you don't take your flower. If you do, you'll kill your love. Your love can't leave the house, so when you want people to meet it, they have to come over. Awesome, are you still with me? One day this residence no longer serves you, but there is your flower. Only your ego would say I need to take this flower with me. If I move it, it might die, but I "love" it. Your heart wants that flower to keep going. This is where the saying, "If you love something, let it go!"

Removing someone's freedom with your words or actions isn't love. Placing limitations on someone's future isn't love. If you love someone so fully, you'll let him or her do whatever needs to be done to be happy. Now apply that to yourself. If you're not doing everything you can do to make yourself happy, how can you possibly extend that to another?

Love isn't based on needs: that reflects codependency. Love isn't based on fear, that's learned behavior. Love isn't based on words. You should never get your self-worth from someone else. Love is based on feelings. When you don't have that feeling when you're completely alone, how could you differentiate that feeling from lust, or limerence? Love is the ultimate freedom for yourself and your partner.

Love is a crucial necessity for survival. Without love, we cannot eat properly. Without love, we won't breathe the right air; without love, we won't focus on our breath. Without love, we won't keep ourselves in a safe shelter. Without love, we won't drink enough water. One could argue that love is the most important necessity for our survival. Our love that we dictate to ourselves through our actions tells us that we are important. If you keep attracting relationships that you aren't properly receiving love in, then take a break from relationships for a while. I'm not talking just romantic relationships, but remove yourself from friendships, family and romance for a while and go deep inside. Any relationship that cannot honor the fact that you need time for yourself is one that you need to detox from anyway. So, don't worry about the guilt someone will try to lay on you. That's another trying to burden you with one's expectations. If one can't see what you're doing as a healthy aspect of your growth, that doesn't say anything about you, it says something about the other person. Don't fall into codependent traps.

When you love yourself fully, then you can attract someone that loves themselves fully. You get the best of both worlds. Don't look for your other half in romance or friendships. You aren't two half souls with half bodies coming together to make one person. You're two people coming together and only coming together if it benefits your life. Like I was saying in a previous chapter of this book, there are two aspects to a relationship-help and harm. If the person in your life isn't making your life better, then he or she is making it worse. There's no in between.

The Universe is in a constant state of flux. Your life should only be aiming to get better and better. So, if you're not in a state of joy, you're not ready for a relationship. If you live life harmoniously and skip through town holding your heart as if keeping the strength from piercing your chest, now, you're ready for that level of love. If you're on that level, then you shouldn't be accepting anything less than that level of self-love from the other person in the relationship whether it's romantic or platonic. Let's get one thing straight: family is a friendship. If your family brings you down and can't accept you and is constantly trying to chip away at you, walk away. You wouldn't let a friend treat you like that. At least I hope you wouldn't. I don't care if you're such strong bloodlines that you're still physically connected giving each other blood transfusions. Find another donor!

What you accept is what you're willing to accept. This might be hard to agree with but once you get it, you get it! If someone is constantly filling the relationship with poison, then you're ingesting poison. You've already decided to eat healthy, drink enough water, exercise, meditate, do Yoga. But why are you still sick? Maybe it's something else you're ingesting? You have to be honest with yourself and look at every circumstance in your life. Is there anywhere that needs healing right now? Is there a relationship that you could do without? Is there a substance that you can do without? Are you distracting yourself with too much stimulus? Are you getting enough sleep? Ask these questions to yourself before going to the doctor. Unless you want to be on medication for the rest of your life. Because to them, that's the end game. There are very few medical doctors who want to heal you. From my experience when I've been sick, I've had to figure it out myself. They blanket bomb you with meds until you stop coming. Most of the time you don't need that medication.

You can heal yourself, and it starts with love and being honest with yourself. Being completely honest with yourself is self-love. We've been taught then when you get in a relationship that it is settling down. Don't believe that. When you find the right relationship, you'll be rising up. Both sides of the relationship will soar. Don't ever settle. Settling isn't practicing self-love.

We constantly focus on our outward appearances physically, mentally, and spiritually. How are the opinions of others affecting you? If someone told you your mother is a horrible person, would you believe this label? Now apply that to anyone else. Everyone's walking around with a perception of what you're going through, a perception of what you feel. Don't remove someone's integrity with your opinion of him or her. You know nothing of one's struggle, nothing of his or her fight.

Sometimes we remove people from our lives to fully heal the wounds. Meanwhile, those wounds were actually inflicted by you believing what they said, condoning what they did. I've been guilty of this. I call it protecting my energy. But really, it's not an act of compassion but cowardice. Sure, if someone tells you, you're horrible person, yeah, we may not want to talk to this person again. In all respects it might be healthy to not talk to him or her again. But your beliefs should not come from another's opinion. It's the same thing if someone says you're beautiful! Of course, it's an amazing thing to hear. But you should know you're beautiful! You shouldn't be looking for that belief from someone else. So, when someone tells you, you're horrible, then you should reply that he or she is wonderful, loving, and kind. Because responding negatively creates more negativity. This is a huge example of where I've gone off track.

How do you get back the vibration you want, the vibration you deserve?... it all stems from compassion. The more compassion you exude, the more you'll attract that compassion back. You're deserving of someone who sees the good in you! You're all deserving of someone who wants the best for you. Sure, people might show you their true colors. But their true colors might not have been received with compassion. Maybe someone is feeding you negativity because he or she has never been fed positivity. Who's feeding you? Are you being fed honestly? If no one's supporting you, that's fine. That doesn't mean you need to reciprocate. Show them more support than they've ever seen.

I'm upset I didn't have this awareness before, and in turn l probably let a lot of people down. I let my hurt, pain and beliefs people had of me run my emotional life. When your emotions are in control, you're not. You control the emotions. You control how you react. It's as simple as that. Don't let someone create the victim inside of you. The Universe is looking out for you if you let it. If someone walks out of your life and doesn't want to talk to you anymore, that's fine. You can always pray that if you were meant to be there for each other, you'll eventually reunite, resolved of any indifference.

In sum, compassion is the highest form of love and with that compassion for yourself; the Mirror Paradox will work to attract compassion back to you. You'll always attract what you are. Be the highest form of love. This resides inside of you. You can heal so many situations with love and compassion. You don't have to have anything in common with someone, or even understand one's situation a little bit to have compassion.

# Chapter 12

## The Mirror Paradox

So, what's the Mirror Paradox? What's a paradox? The Mirror Paradox represents the lenses in which you react to every situation, or in the case in which you're healed on emotional and spiritual levels we don't react to. A paradox is a seemingly absurd statement. So how is the Mirror Paradox seemingly absurd? It's seemingly absurd because we're taught to avoid the conflict that is causing us disease. We're raised that this is unhealthy so you should just leave the situation. I'm saying for the sake of your healing stick around a little longer. Stick around until you become fully conscious of the pattern that emerges. This will be a pattern because sometimes you need to see the same thing happen in multiple relationships before you have the realization that this is the thing that is there to teach you your next lesson in healing. If you don't acknowledge the pattern, it'll keep showing up until you do. You'll continue to attract the situation that shows you the pattern of the unhealed part of your vessel. Every time we have a reaction, the Mirror Paradox is working to our benefit. We react so we know how we need to heal. We react to know where we need to heal. We react so we know exactly where the trigger is. The paradox is people often avoid these triggers from these reactions rather than embrace them as something that's happening for them. It's such a simple concept that requires so much honesty.

When you're triggered by trying to be controlled, you have a control issue. Sure, no one likes being controlled. But when this is just a simple issue with working within your job description in a place of employment, you aren't being controlled. If within working in your job description you get annoyed and triggered over and over again, you need to either find a new job and face the trigger head on and try to acknowledge why you're being triggered and what the root cause of that trigger is. When you avoid these situations that trigger you, you are essentially what spiritual catalysts call "spiritual bypassing". When you bypass and avoid these triggers, the Universe will keep giving you the scenarios repeatedly until you embrace and deal what the root of the problem. If you avoid everyone who triggers you for feeling like you're being controlled, then you'll be avoiding your healing for the rest of your life. What's the root of why you feel like that? Why is this trigger so sensitive to me? A lot of people will make strict boundaries with their partners and friends. This is a really good idea, but in a way sometimes they're way too strict and they never actually deal with the reason of that particular trigger.

I avoided relationships where partners talked down to me. I dodged these relationships for a while thinking these people were just in fact rude and not very compassionate. It was only until I embraced the fact that I'm intelligent and started to accept that I could help people using my intellectual body that I stopped attracting these relationships. The Universe would keep throwing these people at me until I was ready to put my foot down and say enough. I won't take this abuse anymore, and why do I keep attracting people who treat me like I'm stupid? It's because there were still some self-limiting beliefs that I was stupid.

There were self-limiting beliefs that I wasn't a writer. Although I have played in multiple bands for 10 years and probably wrote over thirty songs and numerous poems, I still thought I wasn't a writer. What was my limiting belief stemming from? I did poorly in English classes in high school and a few different teachers said "maybe writing isn't your thing." All of this because I engaged fully in what they were trying to teach me. I was bored, so I thought they must be right. Don't believe anything anyone tells you, ever. They're lying. Even when they tell you, you're an amazing person. You need to have that belief yourself. Don't even believe me.

Let's get back to the Mirror Paradox before I get too off track. Let's say you have a self-limiting belief that you aren't attractive and you want to be confident. Why do you keep attracting people that aren't confident? Like attracts like. I have said it a few times already: we're not magnets. We attract similar frequencies. Our frequency is directly related to how much we love ourselves. The paradox can be so profound but also so simple. When we love ourselves unconditionally, we can attract unconditional love. This is just that simple. Everything we attract is because of how we see and feel about ourselves. When we take care of ourselves, we'll attract people that take care of themselves. It goes on every level on every body that incorporates your vessel. When we take care of ourselves spiritually, we'll attract people who take care of themselves the same amount on the same level.

So, if you're constantly asking yourself, why is this happening to me, you need to change your question to what haven't I seen about myself that needs healing. What am I denying about my healing process that could benefit me to the next level of compassion and unconditional love? Self-love is self-honesty, brutal honesty that cuts to the core of every issue. When you cut to the core of those issues, you create pathways for new solutions to emerge into your life. When these pathways emerge, your truth will flourish as well. There are fewer obstacles in your way and your path will become clearer on a mental level, when the mental level clears up the physical body has more room to breathe and heal on a deeper level. When you breathe deeper, your spiritual body will awaken. When your spiritual body awakens, you start to find your true purpose on this earth. I'll give you a hint: your true purpose isn't working yourself to the point of exhaustion. When you work yourself to a level of exhaustion, you aren't practicing self-love. Every trigger will be a window to where you need to heal. When you get upset, you should be grateful for being upset. When this moment arises, it's showing you in that exact form and point of reference, this is a problem that you're ignoring. Embrace these moments they are beautiful and beneficial growth moments. Don't get frustrated with yourself for being upset either. Just say, "Hey, wow I lost my cool there." Forgive yourself. You had an imperfect moment, a human moment. Consciousness is conscious awareness. You're aware of every moment or at least strive to be.

This is what living in the moment is. You're consciously aware of every moment as it's happening. You aren't focused on the past. You aren't thinking about the future. You're in the moment fully, embracing every second as a new gift for your development. What a gift you get to receive being in the moment. I get to be present and fully embrace every second of my life. You walk down the street, you get to embrace every step, every breath, and all the things happening around you. You get to co-create when you're present. When you think about what's going to happen in two days, two weeks, or two years you aren't co-creating that moment you're living in right NOW. You focus on something that isn't happening so hard that you miss the magic that happens for you.

When I live in the moment, I notice numerology. It's constantly happening, showing me numbers in repetition. Everywhere I go there are sequences of number popping up: on license plates, signs, phone numbers, they're everywhere. This is the Universe reiterating, "Hey, we notice you are paying attention. So, we are going to let you know we are paying attention to you too". These miracles happen every day when you live in the moment. Sometimes I burst out in laughter when I notice the synchronicities the Universe is showing me. In those moments it is very hard to deny a higher force at play. That higher force is in direct communication with me. What a miracle!

Let's get back to the triggers and the healing. Everything ties so intricately together between all your bodies. Your physical body sends electrical signals through your mental body. These electrical signals are part of your light body. Your light body speaks directly to your spiritual body, your soul. Your soul is both connected to your body and everything else in the Universe on the most intricate levels. All of these bodies work in unison and create the most amazing system in the Universe. The human soul and body working together is the most powerful force the Universe has. We are all miracles! These triggers that we ignore will get stuck in one of these bodies of our vessel. Manifesting in dis-ease. The Chakras and Nadis are the intersecting points of these bodies where the electrical energy travels through all of these bodies in our vessel.

Ever been to Yoga and had an emotional release from a deep stretch? Do you wonder why you cried when you stretched your hips or why you had such a relief of weight off your shoulders when you stretched your back? These energetic pathways become blocked and clogged. Science is now finally understanding and acknowledging these ideals. Many hospitals are incorporating Reiki and other holistic energetic practices into the healing process. We're at a cusp of a great spiritual shift where people can start to understand and embrace that there's so much more going on in our vessels than previously thought and taught about.

When we avoid these triggers and causes of disease, we're essentially stopping the electrical signal from being able to go through our body; thus, we're causing the dis-ease. When we can be honest and look for the solution as to why these things are happening for us, it's the most cathartic thing we can do. Sometimes these things are far beyond what we could have even imagined in the terms of the reason why we have that particular blockage. We have to realize we cannot fully heal ourselves without help. If you have mental problems, you see a counselor or psychologist. Sometimes those problems, triggers or blocks will be of the spiritual sense.

To illustrate, I was spinning my wheels when I was dealing with crippling depression and anxiety. I could intuit the needs of people so well I'd be able to tell the counselor exactly what she needed to hear to make her think she was helping me. I didn't realize at the time, but I was spiritually bypassing. I didn't need a counselor at that time I needed to stop avoiding my feelings. It wasn't until I started meditating regularly and seeking the wisdom of spiritual professionals both meditators and Reiki Masters that I started to see results. The more and more I read yogic texts and was honest with myself, the more healing occurred.

I remember going to a psychologist and he asked me about the history of mental dis-ease in my family. I told him avoidance. He looked and me shocked and kind of bewildered. He said "avoidance?" I said, "Yes, avoidance. There are a lot of mental problems in my family on both sides and I am the first person in my family to say there is something wrong." At this point in my life there was no more denying that there was an issue that needed resolving. I had talked to both my parents about my mental health issues and saw a pattern emerge. My father told me he never struggled with mental health. Now I'm no dummy. My father is a high functioning alcoholic. If you're an alcoholic at all, it's because you're in denial and avoidance of some deep dark truths. So, it was obvious to me that the pattern that had emerged from both sides of my family was a pattern of avoidance of dealing with the real issues at hand.

One year I had lost two uncles in the family. One uncle on each side of the family died within 3 days of each other, both due to smoking. My uncle on my mom's side had cancer in his mouth from smoking his entire adult life. My mom asked me if I wanted to go visit him in the hospital in Winnipeg, Manitoba. I asked if he was doing anything to help his situation. She told me he was still drinking and smoking and refused to quit. In my lower state of understanding, I said, "I don't want to visit him if he isn't even going to try to survive and make the best of his situation." That was something that haunted me and bugged me for a long time. I needed to make peace with that situation and luckily was blessed with being able to at a spiritual ceremony years later.

At the time I was no better. In fact, I was still in passive suicide mode. I was still drinking daily thinking that I had my life figured out. I was in complete denial that I had a problem. I stopped drinking probably thirty-three times before I stopped drinking. Each time I told myself, "This is the last drink I'm going to consume." In my elitist mentality, I thought I was somehow better than my uncle, that I was somehow taking care of myself better. That mental pattern embodied a load of lies that just weren't true. I'm very fortunate I'm mature enough to have the realization about all of this. Just writing about this situation brings up emotions of sadness and regret signaling that there is still some healing to do. This is an amazing reminder to not forget the things that happened. Dwell on the memories of the past. But not in a self-deprecation that enables your victim mentality kind of way. Dwell on your memories so you can come to peace with why these things happened and why you felt the way you did. All of these things are amazing stories and intricate pieces to the puzzle of your healing.

Your reality will become the product of your thoughts and efforts. I contemplated writing this book for months and months, but without typing anything down my thoughts weren't actually manifesting into anything. You need to do the work. This has been my biggest lesson in life. I'd attract people with the most amazing potential and dreams. We'd share with each other what we wanted to become and accomplish in our lives, but I'd continually find myself frustrated that these people weren't doing the work. The truth was *I* wasn't doing the work either. Everything that would start to be the work would turn into distractions. I am a very easily distracted person. So, doing the work for me was very extreme. Before I started facing and seeing my true north, I needed to sell my couch, TV, iPad, furniture, excess dishes, and everything that I had surplus of in my life. I cleared my external clutter out so I could stop making decisions that were really distractions.

Sometimes our healing is beyond our realm of what we could have imagined was possible. I own a house and in the transitional period between being a Journey-person electrician and the spiritual awakening I found myself very distraught about the idea of the home. I was constantly worried about owning the house and paying the bills. It was quite irrational to think about really. I'd owned the house for almost eight years by the time this phobia showed up. I'd already been paying the bills and done extensive renovations to the home.

In my awakening journey, I fell upon past lives. During my physiotherapy, I was seeing a counselor multiple times a week. In this process I had severe anxiety and depression that was crippling my abilities to go shopping and be in public. It was to a point that I couldn't even handle being in a grocery store. I lost weight because I was anxious buying groceries. During one of my physio counseling sessions, my counselor offered to try doing a past life regression. I was very open to the idea as at this point, as I was already seeking out holistic energy healing to try to desperately help my situation. I think this one event was a catalyst for my major spiritual awakening that pursued subsequently.

I went back to a previous life where I was in a French hospital. There was a long black-haired woman sitting to my right and it was a private room. I could describe the room so vividly I could draw it. In the past life regression, the hypnotherapist asks a lot of questions to try to get you to intuitively figure out where and who you were. I came to the conclusion that I was my grandfather Frank. My grandfather died many years before I was born, probably 17 years to ballpark it. At the end of the regression, I said, "I am my grandfather, Frank." At that precise moment my kundalini awoke and my body was shaking and reverberating uncontrollably. I was in shock. This was my first conscious experience with my kundalini. I didn't know at the time that this was a kundalini awakening but once I had talked to my Reiki Master, I had figured it out.

After this point in time, I started meditating religiously. I tried many past life regressions and figured out I was quite Clairvoyant. I'd inquired with my soul before doing another past life regression off of YouTube. I'd asked for guidance regarded why I struggled dealing with the ownership of my house. Why does owning a property affect me so deeply? In this particular regression, I found myself in France in what I'd been told through Claircognizance was the 1850s. I owned a vineyard in France. I lived there with my wife and was very successful. I fast forwarded twenty years to see that I'd been killed. I enquired to why I'd been killed and only after returning to this life; again, I realized that I'd been killed for my land, so I was so reluctant to sell. After doing research I found that during the time period of the 1850s, Bordeaux wine became a very popular and expensive export in France. Thus, making the land and vineyards quite profitable. I'd gone back far enough through my soul's memories to discover the root of why I experienced so much anxiety owning a property. The irrational fear was a real fear attached to a past life. Had I not seen this with my third eye, I wouldn't have believed it to be possible. After this, things started to really change for me. I've now seen over a dozen of my past lives in relation to part of my life that needed healing at the time.

When you have a car that breaks and you don't have the tools to fix it properly, you take it to a mechanic. You consult a capable professional. The same goes for any dis-ease that you cannot figure out yourself. Trust me you can't figure it all out yourself. I've been fortunate to be intertwined in the holistic community knowing many psychics, energy healers, meditation facilitators, and life coaches. I've called upon many people to help give me the missing piece to my healing that my ego was blocking me from seeing. Trust me, your ego will get in your way. Make these connections with the healers that resonate with you. When you start to see the synchronicities, more will happen. Then right away your life will be only synchronicities. It will be all miracles. Every event that happens will be a miracle. From your keys getting stuck in your ignition to getting kicked out of your place to live. The Universe is kind, and society wants you to be in fear mode to feed the consumerism machine. Don't succumb to the fear. Embrace that you can be in control of any fears by facing them head on!

# Chapter 13

## Using the Mirror Paradox

How do we effectively use the Mirror Paradox? For one, we need to not spiritually bypass the situations that are going to show us where to heal. Don't avoid a situation for a trigger. Every trigger will show you how you feel inside. The triggers are the road map to healing the issue deep down inside. We use the Mirror Paradox by being honest. This brutal honesty will show us our truth. In that truth we'll know what we like and what we don't like. If you want to attract better, you have to be better.

The Universe is a giant mirror. It reflects everything back to us so we can see ourselves. How we are treated by others impacts how we see ourselves. This giant mirror reflects back everything. If you give a weird body language, you get it back. If you exhibit negative emotions, you get them back. If you aren't giving out the emotion the mirror is showing you, then you don't like being treated that way. This giant mirror is so intuitive that it shows you any and all areas that require your attention. So, when you're in a state of bliss embrace it and be grateful for it.

I was in a Yoga class the other day and at the very end we were laying in Shavasana. While lying in the corpse pose, I was trying to focus on the music. This class was in an older building so room noises flooded from one room to another. I could hear a guy singing quite loudly. After about a minute I found myself getting annoyed. But before I could get more annoyed, I remembered the Mirror Paradox. I told myself why are you trying to control this? Why does this only have to be a certain frequency to relax? The problem wasn't the guy singing. *I* was the problem. I was the one who needed to release that control tendency and just focus on myself. The Mirror Paradox showed me this. Being in the present moment in every moment made it so I can have this realization.

Many people who have been very traumatized will likely say, "Yah, but you can't just focus and ignore the trauma?" In a way they're right. But this is also in fact giving your power away to the trauma. If you really want to heal it you will meditate. If you really are that triggered everywhere you go, you'll seek psychological help. If you keep giving your power to the trauma of course it's going to stay. Don't be fooled by someone saying you're broken, and you won't heal from this. These are people who are also brainwashed to believe everything they are told. If you put in the work finding new neuropathways you will help rewire the brain to start firing the way it needs to again. When the brain can fire in a happy state, you can use different pathways for the positive things to travel around in your brain. Shamans and medicine healers around the world have known this for a long time. They used natural medicines to help people go on spirit quests, and soul journeys. A lot of this was done as preventative medicine to prepare cultures for adulthood. Why was major depression not a huge problem in the past? Because people would seek out spiritual help.

All in all, don't let your emotions give things value. Don't value silence, don't value noise. You'll create these limits for your happiness. If you can only value listening to a certain kind of music and you constantly distract yourself by listening to music, one day it's not going to work and you will be upset. Healing is in a lot of music. Healing is also in silence. Remember what I was saying before we didn't have music readily available over 90 years ago?  Compared to the timeline of human evolution, this is a pin drop in time. So, have we evolved so fast that we can now be constantly distracted? I don't think so. We don't change as a species that rapidly. If we want to go inward, we have to cut out the external distractions. When we cut out the distractions, we get the messages. Messages always come in the silence.

Watch the mirror in life and you'll see how the Universe is always showing you yourself! When you go around smiling at everyone, you'll get smiles back, as these are other people aware of the mirror. They might not even be consciously aware, but on a subconscious level they know about the mirror. The Mirror Paradox is very real and it happens every day in every situation. When you are generous and kind, you'll get generosity and kindness. When you raise your vibration to a higher level, you'll attract those higher vibrations from other people. Be so happy that grumpy sad negative people won't even want to be around you. The Universe will shift people out of your way. I remember being so happy at certain times that it would turn people right off. They'd ask, "What are you so happy about?" Why am I not happy? I have everything I need in life. All the other stuff is on its way to me right now. There's no reason to not be happy. When your basic needs are met, there are some amazing blessings!

# Chapter 14

## Conclusion

Now that I've shared my journey with you, I hope it empowers you. I hope this quest is a catalyst for your growth and understanding. There was so much hardship in this story, but in all of that pain I found what I truly needed, growth. When you honor yourself, you get to be yourself and love yourself. This is the miracle I hope you take from this book. When you release everything that you've been taught and learned, you get to see who you really are inside. You're so much more complex. You aren't "Frank the guy who has a van." You get to define yourself on a way deeper level. You can create who you want to be with that truth. You can then be the deeply spiritual being, having profound experiences every day in life.

Tune into yourself fully. When you tune in, you can be so present in every moment you won't miss anything. Don't focus on what might happen or what has happened. Be so present that you get to witness every breath as a gift of life. This is a gift you get to receive; and when you receive these gifts, it gives you and amazing feeling of gratitude. Be grateful for everything. If you have a roof over your head and don't go to bed hungry, you're so blessed. You get to sleep comfortably. You get to breathe. You get to eat. In this day and age, you can eat whatever foods you want. The Universe will always give you reasons to be grateful when you're grateful. Use the Mirror Paradox to reflect back more opportunities for gratitude every day. You'll see there are always more reasons to be thankful than there are reasons to complain. All of this happens for you. Everything will always align to show you how blessed you are. Seeing that you're blessed is up to you though. You have to be the one to realize that you're receiving so much every day!

I hope you have learned through my struggles that the clutter in your life isn't necessary. When you clear out your physical world, you clean out your internal world as well. The level of your commitment to being happy is dependent on how much you clear out from your world both mentally and physically. Without all the clutter, you purge your mind for the spiritual experience. This is the most amazing experience you can have. Embrace the fact that we're all spiritual beings and taking care of the being is just as important as taking care of the physical and mental being in your vessel as well. They all work in unison whether its harmony or disharmony is up to you.

Remember society's two monsters. Don't get trapped by consumerism and then consumed by debt. These two things aren't necessary evils that need to plague you. Living within your means is not only intelligent, but it's also humble, and sustainable. So, embrace your humility. Embrace your intelligence. You know better, you're smarter than that. Stop making excuses. Make yourself the biggest priority!

Practice self-love. You'll receive so many miracles. Embrace every amazing thing that happens for you. This is the Universe shining its blessings on you for you to be able to thrive in life. When you embrace the miracles, you'll acknowledge the miracles. The Universe really likes that. It'll throw more miracles at you. Start calling everything a miracle. Even if people think you're crazy. Let them. If I wake up, well rested, and feeling good I call it a miracle. It's a miracle we have a stove to make morning tea on. It's a miracle there's so much technology to help us get to work on time. It's a miracle we can go buy whatever we want from the grocery store to eat at any time. They're all miracles. Don't just call things miracles either, you have to believe it. See and feel and acknowledge and you'll receive more!

Again, I want you to remember that you're all empaths. You get amazing gifts if you should choose to use them. Awakening the spiritual body will give you access to some or all of these gifts. You are all psychic, you are all Clairvoyant. Every one of you has amazing gifts that you should embrace. Having these gifts and using them has changed my life. Imagine being so Claircognizant that you can show compassion to anyone in any situation. This is a real superpower. Talk about being able to receive someone fully? Not only can you listen to someone, you can understand others. You'll be able to be there for people more. The world can shift to a higher level of compassion. This vibration will help make people realize their faults and take steps to heal them in more responsible ways. That's what all of this is about: healing in a responsible and communal way.

Remember that good versus bad will hold you back. Release all of these notions. Nothing is good and nothing is bad. It's just what it is. You need to stop the labels and practice radical acceptance. When we practice that, we can choose to be happy. We'll no longer look for the circumstance that will set us free. Radical acceptance will set you free from ever having to think the world is out to get you. It will help you get out of victim mentality and start repairing the trauma that has been hardwired in your brain. You all deserve to live a happy healthy life. You can't really be healthy on every level if you aren't happy. So, accept the things that happen. Things happen, and they happen to show you how you're reacting to them. By accepting, you can stop the reaction from occurring; thus, you can take your emotions into control and keep them in control. You deserve to be in control of your own life. You should be happy!

Remember what we need to survive. We've been led astray when it comes to our basic needs. You need food, water, air, shelter, and love. Don't forget that. You deserve all of those things. Everyone deserves all of those things. When you know your worth, you'll be worth receiving all of these things. You need to give love to receive love. You need to love yourself to be able to give love. It's such an important but simple idea. When you love someone fully and there are no conditions attached to that love, they can walk out of your life at any moment and you'll still love them. Unconditional love is an amazing gift you can give. You can't teach someone what it is if you don't practice it. So, if you're still attracting relationships when you're expected to change or there are conditions to the relationship. There's still some healing you need to do with yourself. These are all signs using the Mirror Paradox that you need to love yourself more, without condition, without expectation.

Have faith that there's always room for improvement, being aware and not letting your emotions run your life is how you stay conscious of where that improvement needs to take place. So, go out and poor love into everything you experience and encounter in life. Make love to life as they'd say, and you'll attract someone who is on the same level.  If someone attacks you verbally, respond with unconditional love. He or she could be very hurt but don't let another person's hurt affect you and bring you down. Don't ever meet someone on his or her level. Showing reciprocity with how people treat you is immature and it's a form of spiritual bypassing. Instead of rising above, you sink down. Don't do that anymore, you are better than that. But with that being said, there are absolutely no circumstances in life where you need to lower yourself to others. It doesn't matter who they are. No parent, sibling, spouse, friend, or acquaintance should ever lower your self-esteem. If they can't support your choices in life you just leave. When they say no, you say next. Walk away from toxic relationships. Walk away from negativity. If it doesn't serve, you leave it.

In closing, the time to empower yourself is right now. Write down what you want in life and don't accept anything else. Your life will change so dramatically. At first a bunch of toxic waste will dispel from your life. But once the old doors are closed, you'll have room for true friends' true

family. Until you set those standards, you're telling
the Universe how you want to be treated. You
never get what you want: you get what you are.
Hold your head up high and treat yourself well
first. This is where your shift will start. If someone
can't respect your choices, you walk away. If
someone can't treat you to your standards, you
walk away. This is the most basic form of
protecting your energy but also the most crucial.
Lessons in life aren't always easy, but the hardest
lessons bring the most blessings.

As I mentioned, the Universe is the most
powerful mirror. Everything you do will reflect
back. Your actions will reflect back in the actions of
others. Your thoughts will manifest the
circumstances you get to encounter. If you get
annoyed by someone's body language, it's time to
check your own and be perfectly aware of how you
portray yourself. If you don't like how someone
talks to you, check in and see how you talk to that
person or others. Maybe the problem is you're
taking things way too personal? Who cares how
someone talks to you? When you attract better
situations, you won't have to worry about those
people talking to you anymore. They will either
change and their behavior will be more acceptable
or you will vibrate right out of their life. Either way
the problem will be solved.

Tune into this mirror. Use this mirror to
your advantage. This mirror will help you heal on

every level. Even when you can't fully heal yourself, it'll show you there's something to heal. Then you can go to someone who can help you heal. Your body will talk to you, learn to listen. When you learn to quite your mind you can essentially listen to your body. Go meditate, go to Yoga classes. There are a myriad of reasons people get addicted to these classes. They become addicted to feeling good. They get addicted to being in control of their life. Yoga and meditation are so empowering. This is such a healthy feeling. When I look back at the synchronous events that led me to Yoga, they reiterate a miracle. The stars aligned to help me start taking care of myself. Had I not been on this path, I'd still be struggling with depression. When I started mediation on a regular basis, my anxiety practically disappeared.

Learn to hold space for yourself and you'll attract two things: the first is other people willing to be able to hold space for themselves to harness healthy relationships with; the second is you will be able to be receptive to others that need help being heard. You'll open up yourself to your natural healer abilities and benefit everyone around you.

Someone once asked me, "What does it mean to be seen? I was told I need to be seen. How can I be seen?" I replied, "You need to be more vulnerable. The healer in all of us is capable of helping others  When you're vulnerable, you show others your scars. When you show others your scars, you're essentially saying, see, it's normal to be hurt. I was hurt and I healed. Vulnerability is a catalyst for people opening up to you. By being vulnerable, you aren't hiding the work you had to do to be healed. You're proud of the work and willing to show someone the way!"

I hope this book gives you your own moments of realization through the stories of my healing journey. I'm eternally grateful for everyone who reads this and embraces what they find in it to be resonant with their truth.

# Acknowledgments

I would like to thank my family and friends who supported me through the toughest times of my life. I Would like to give a very special thanks to my Reiki Grand Master and friend Quinn Straza. Thank you, Quinn, for showing up in such a synchronistic way in my life when I needed you the most. Thank you to all of the teachers and students that showed up in my life. Thank you to all the angels and ascended masters that converse with me and constantly send me messages.

I would like to give a special Thanks to Sara Derksen. Thank for the contribution to editing and the artwork for the cover of this book. You have been an intricate part of my life throughout my spiritual journey.

Lastly, I would like to give thanks to Stacy Shaneyfelt for the incredible and authentic editing to this book. I am very fortunate to have your expertise with this project.

# About the Editor

Stacy Shaneyfelt

After obtaining her BS in Secondary English Education and MA in English from Slippery Rock University of PA, Stacy embarked on a successful teaching career that spanned public, government, and charter schools in Pittsburgh, PA, Oklahoma City, Norman, OK, and Okinawa, Japan. Stacy earned a 2004 Fulbright-Hays Seminar Scholarship to Thailand and Vietnam from the United States Department of Education as well as Site Teacher of the Year (2009-2010) from Moore Public Schools, Moore Public Schools' District Teacher of the Year Finalist (2009-2010), South Oklahoma City Chamber of Commerce's 2009 Teacher of the Year First Runner-Up, and Longfellow Middle School's Site Teacher of the Year (2006-2007)

In addition to multicultural and social activism, Stacy lives with her awesome husband, two fierce and fabulous daughters, and two frisky fur babies. Stacy now works as a virtual freelancer, private English and ESL tutor, online editor/proofreader, and blogger at Upwork.com, BrainMass.com, and Wyzant.com. Stacy enjoys films, coffee, art, and all things mindful!

## About the Artist

Sara Derksen is a professional Tattoo artist by trade. She is also a Reiki Practitioner. She works with a lot of different types of media doing visual art. Sara is a gifted poet and self-taught through many aspects of spiritualism. She is an aspiring Buddhist. Sara's passions directly align with her work. She offers compassion pricing on self-harm scar tattoo cover ups and is always willing to help someone in need. For custom artwork you can email her directly or if you are ever in Regina, Saskatchewan, go get a tattoo. Her email is Derksen.tattoos@gmail.com

# About the Author

Franklyn Morrison is a Reiki Practitioner and spiritual blogger. A self-employed energy healer by day, and writer by night. His passion for helping others heal is shown through the studies of Yoga, religion and all things spiritual. Having recovered from PTSD through different spiritual practices he hopes to show others the way. Franklyn's desire is to show everyone their true gifts. He is also a medium and a channel for spirits. Franklyn has an enthusiasm for all things in the metaphysical world.

Made in the USA
Middletown, DE
21 December 2019